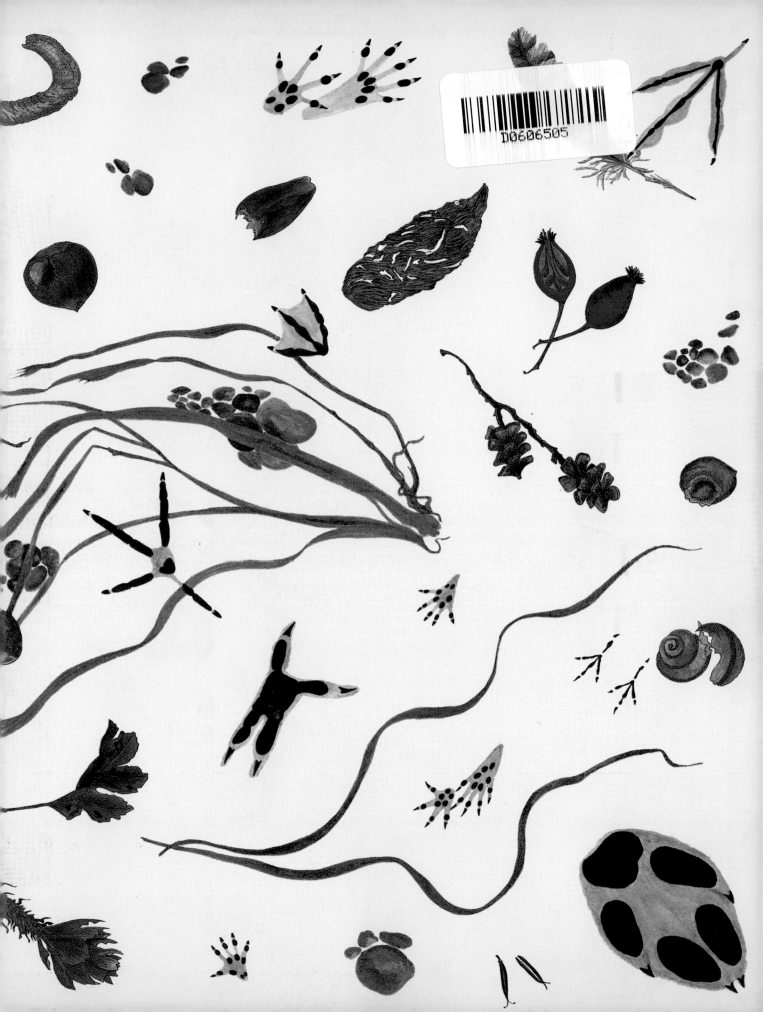

WINTER SURVIVAL

Dedicated to my family with all my love

WINTER SURVIVAL

Nature's Ways of Coping with the Cold

MARI FRIEND

BLANDFORD

ACKNOWLEDGEMENTS

I would like to thank my family and friends for their loving support and encouragement throughout my work on this book. This has been particularly important to me at times when there have been deadlines to be met; when my eyes have been feeling the strain of close work; and when my wild garden has been calling me outdoors. Thank you too to Mr R A Murray of the Leeds Weather Centre for being so willing to read through my draft chapter on winter weather, and for his valuable comments.

A BLANDFORD BOOK
First published in the UK in 1993 by Blandford
An Imprint of Cassell
Villiers House
41/47 Strand
LONDON WC2N 5JE

Distributed in Australia by
Capricorn Link (Australia) Pty Ltd
P.O. Box 665, Lane Cove, NSW 2066

British Library Cataloguing in Publication Data
A catalogue record for this book is available from the British Library

ISBN 0 7137 2348 3

Produced and designed by
SAVITRI BOOKS LTD
115J Cleveland Street
London WC1P 5PN

Art direction and design by Mrinalini Srivastava
Edited by Caroline Taggart

Typeset in Garamond Stempel by Dorchester Typesetting Group Ltd
Produced by Mandarin Offset, printed and bound in Hong Kong

CONTENTS

PREFACE

Nature can be very harsh. Plants and animals have to withstand the heat of the hottest desert, the freezing cold of the polar regions, the competition of the rainforests and the pressure of the deepest oceans. Some of these creatures are tiny and delicate – so how do they do it?

The answer is that, over millions of years, plants and animals that have to live in extreme conditions of any kind have adapted. That is, they have found ways of coping with heat, cold, drought or whatever their local problem might be. In this book, I take a look at some of the principles behind the adaptations which enable life to survive a cold period in an otherwise temperate climate.

In my recent book, *Small Wonder*, I touched on the subject of winter survival in a chapter of that name. But here I have been able to expand on the theme and produce some illustrations which will perhaps draw you from your cosy fireside and out into your local park or into the countryside in the deep midwinter. I hope this book will encourage you to see winter as I see it – austere beauty at every turn, with each shred of colour a promise that spring will indeed return.

The plants, animals and habitats described in *Winter Survival* are spread over Britain, Europe and North America, wherever winter causes hardship in nature. Obviously the severity of winter differs enormously between northern Norway and southern Spain, but even in Spain there are mountainous areas where conditions are cold enough for bears to hibernate. I have tried to cover as wide a range of countries and creatures as possible, while still sharing with you the fascination of the animals I observe from my kitchen window. I have searched moorland, mountains, rivers, lakes, seashores, woodland, hedgerows and fields as well as gardens and their small ponds to find ways in which nature copes with the yearly chill.

Many of us are able to watch the behaviour of garden birds throughout the winter and even help some of them to survive their ordeal; but what about the birds that choose to overwinter in the sun – how do they manage the journey and how do they find their way back in spring? And where do all the insects go? Many of them are short-lived and die before the cold weather sets in, leaving their eggs to hatch in spring and ensure the survival of the species; but what about the ones with longer lifespans? In this book, I look at the remarkable ways in which insects and other animals can put their lives on hold until the warmer weather comes.

Winter Survival explores the phenomenon of autumn colour and leaf fall; camouflage in the snow; congregations of animals that find safety in numbers; and flowers that bloom despite the cold weather. You can find out about the varying degrees of hibernation and the hazards of overwintering in water; and you can learn to read the tracks and signs that animals leave in the snow.

Plants and animals are a vital part of the life on our planet. That means that their survival is essential for our future, and the future of our children. I hope this book will give you some ideas about the importance of preserving habitats as well as enable you to share the delight I take in watching nature perform her wonders.

PREPARING FOR WINTER

Spring is the season of rebirth and renewal; summer brings warmth and plenty; autumn has splendid maturity with its wealth of fruits; then comes bleak winter, spreading a dreary hue over the land. As the last of autumn's glory silently fades and falls in the chill November wind, the bleak landscape waits in expectant stillness for winter to creep over it. The silence is broken only by the occasional sound of a startled bird.

SHORT DAY – LONG NIGHT

As temperatures fall, so do the leaves. For centuries, country people have watched the behaviour of trees in autumn closely and used it to predict the following winter's weather: 'October with green leaves means a severe winter' is one of many pieces of folk wisdom, most of which seem to spread gloom and despondency. I expect this is because few of us look forward to the short days, long nights and cold of the winter. But when the rich colours of summer begin to dissipate in autumn, there is a burst of splendour as green leaves change to gold, orange, russet or deep crimson. Some trees are more beautiful in autumn than at any other time of the year, their lofty crowns reminding us of the brilliant colour of captured sunsets or perhaps the flickering fires of frosty nights.

But why do so many trees change their leaf colour in autumn, and why do the leaves then fall? The answer lies with the invisible biological clock that all plants and animals have. It measures the length of the day – or night. So, at the spring equinox, when day and night are the same length, plants and animals know that it is time to grow or breed, because a long cold period has just passed and the days are lengthening. At the autumn equinox, after a season of growth and fruitfulness, the days are shortening and it is time to prepare for winter. For many trees, as we shall see, this means losing their leaves. Throughout Britain, Europe and North America all broad-leaved trees and a few coniferous ones such as larches and deciduous cypresses (*Taxodium* spp.) shed their leaves in autumn.

Many small creatures may be found among fallen leaves. Some, such as earthworms and woodlice, are decomposers which feed on the leaves; others, including centipedes and spiders, are predators which hunt the decomposers.

As a matter of interest, in towns and cities where trees grow close to street lights, you may notice that the lamps effectively increase the day length for the trees growing close to them. In other words, the trees do not realize that winter is upon them and they cling on to their leaves longer than trees unaffected by artificial light.

All land plants release water vapour into the air by a process called transpiration. This can take place from any exposed part of the plant, but the greatest water loss is through the pores in the leaves which are known as stomata. The rate of transpiration varies according to atmospheric conditions and the make-up of the plant.

At times, this loss of water can be very harmful. In winter, for example, low ground temperatures make it difficult for a root system to extract water from the soil. If the tree had still to maintain a vast number of leaves with all the evaporation and transpiration this entails, its tissues would quickly dry out and die. So the only way a plant can help itself is to drop its leaves. The first step in this process is that which causes the change in colour.

THE WONDER OF AUTUMN COLOUR

The green colour we see in plants is caused by two closely related pigments, chlorophyll 'a' and chlorophyll 'b'. These pigments are only able to form in the presence of light, with a favourable temperature – not lower than 2°C (36°F) or higher than 40°C (104°F) – and with an adequate supply of water and minerals from the soil and carbohydrates manufactured by the plant. You can prove these points by putting a houseplant away into the darkness of a fridge or a hot airing cupboard and not watering it; but beware, the plant may never be the same again!

Chlorophyll in living cells is necessary for the process called photosynthesis to take place. This is the method by which plants manufacture organic foods from simple inorganic compounds using light energy. The other essential factors for photosynthesis are sunlight, carbon dioxide and water. The process produces oxygen, carbohydrates and water vapour, all of which are essential for life on earth.

In autumn, when the days become shorter and temperatures fall, a layer of specialized cells begins to form at the base of each deciduous leaf. The cells behind this layer become corky and impervious to water. The normal transportation of materials in and out of the leaf is impeded, and this interferes with the formation of chlorophyll. Chlorophyll is constantly being used up, and when the supplies required for its renewal run out, the leaves lose their green colour. When the green pigment disappears, any other colouring which may be in the leaves can be seen. Yellow chemicals called flavenoids are always found in association with chlorophyll in leaves, protecting the chlorophyll from too much sunlight; so when the green colour is no longer produced, the yellow becomes visible. Trees such as sycamore, birch, horse chestnut, black poplar and its hybrids have predominantly yellow leaves in autumn.

Some leaves also contain anthocyanins, chemical compounds which give the colours red, blue and violet-purple. These colours are not usually present in the leaf during the summer, as flavenoids are, but form as the leaves begin to wilt. Often the leaves which develop the greatest intensity of red are rich in sugars. These show up particularly well on bright autumn days after a cold snap, as frost traps the sugars in the leaves. This explains why some trees which have red leaves in autumn are particularly spectacular in certain years; look out for Virginia creeper, maples such as red maple and silver maple, sumachs and some oaks, especially pin oak and scarlet oak. In New England, where early frosts followed by warm spells commonly occur and deciduous trees are abundant, the glorious reds of autumn are rightly famous. The forests of Canada are spectacular, too. I revelled in these one autumn, then returned home to Britain, where the golden leaves of the beeches and the yellow needles of the larches were just as lovely, if less flamboyant.

The presence of these colourful chemicals may also be detected in fruits, where chlorophyll is eliminated in the same way as it is from leaves. Yellow flavenoids and other orange and yellow substances called carotenoids become dominant in lemons, grapefruits, pears, apricots, oranges and rosehips, which all glow with bright colour when they are ripe and ready to leave the tree. Blackberries, blackcurrants and elderberries are red-purple when they are ripe – if you have ever picked them, you will have found that the pigment stains your fingers.

THE FALL

Let us return to the specialized cells which form at the base of each deciduous leaf, causing the colour to change.

The cells form a layer across the area where the leaf stalk joins the twig. This is called the abscission layer. The cells nearest the twig make a corky layer and those nearest the leaf stalk are thin and loosely packed. The valuable carbohydrates which have been manufactured in the leaf are in soluble form and are normally passed from the leaf into the plant through the vascular tissue.

the last of the autumn fruits

Waste substances pass from the plant into the leaf for excretion. Gradually the abscission layer thickens and blocks the vascular tissue, so that water and minerals are no longer able to enter the leaf from the plant. The leaf changes colour and begins to die.

The cells in the leaf stalk degenerate and the vascular strands, which once carried the plant's water supplies into the leaf and the carbohydrates out, finally break, so that the leaf falls. The corky layer of cells near the twig now protects the plant from water loss and prevents disease-producing organisms from entering the plant.

The shape of the scar left by the fallen leaf is specific to a given species of plant. For example, the horse chestnut tree is so called because the scar left by a fallen leaf is horseshoe-shaped; the vein scars even leave marks that look like the nails of the shoe. You will find leaf scars on all twigs; those of horse chestnut, sweet chestnut, ash and sycamore are probably the easiest to examine.

EVERGREENS

Some trees have evolved ways of solving the problem of water loss, so they do not need to shed their leaves in autumn. These trees have become 'evergreen'. Evergreen conifers such as pine and spruce have small, needle-shaped leaves with thick skins and only a few sunken stomata which retain water very efficiently; holly, yew, laurel and mistletoe have tough leaves with thick, waxy, protective skins. Next time you go for a walk in the park or the countryside, feel the difference between a deciduous leaf and an evergreen one, by taking an evergreen leaf in one hand and a deciduous leaf in the other. You will see that the evergreen leaf is thick and shiny and the deciduous leaf is thin and matt.

Evergreens keep their leaves for an indefinite period, but the older leaves are shed at some time during the year.

Long ago, in the days of our ancient ancestors, when the winters were long, cold and hungry, any plant which retained its leaves was regarded with esteem. Many trees lost their leaves and to all intents and purposes 'died', but there were those few wonderful species which remained green and so gave the promise that vegetation would return to life with the lengthening days.

horse chestnut

In the days before Christianity spread through Europe, there was a cult of tree worship which took many forms. The followers of this cult believed that trees were the home of powerful spirits, and their worship was associated with fertility. The practice of giving the revered tree offerings, in fulfilment of or in accordance with a vow, lingered for a long time after the arrival of Christianity, particularly among the Slavic and Teutonic peoples.

Remnants of the tree cult can still be found in various guises, notably in Roman art of the first century AD, disseminated across Europe in carvings of wood and stone and subtly portrayed in churches of the thirteenth, fourteenth and fifteenth centuries. These carvings have various designs, but the main feature is usually a human (sometimes an animal) head, peering through foliage which issues through the mouth and often the eyes and ears. These foliate heads may be found carved in stone on corbels, capitals, fonts, lintels and tombs, and in wood on misericords, screens and the ends of pews. They are said to depict the 'Green Man' or 'Jack-in-the-Green', the symbol of the renewal of life in spring. Some people believe the carvings represent tree spirits or demons, illustrating the continuance of tree worship at the time of their carving; others feel that the heads show the inextricable link between man and tree, held together in a natural cycle of death and rebirth.

Until quite recently, people would gather in the abbey ruins at Glastonbury, in the south-west of England, on Old Christmas Eve (5 January) to watch for the first buds of the Glastonbury thorn tree, *Crataegus praecox*, to open. The original thorn tree is supposed to have been planted in Glastonbury by Joseph of Arimathea, who allowed Jesus to be buried in his family tomb after the Crucifixion. Legend tells us that when St Joseph reached Glastonbury on a mission to bring Christianity to Britain, he struck his staff into the slope of Weary-all Hill, outside the town, and the dead wood immediately burst into flower. Thereafter it was said to blossom every year at the time of Christ's birth. There are three specimens of this early flowering thorn tree in Glastonbury today: one stands in front of the parish church, one in the grounds of the ruined abbey and the third on Weary-all Hill.

Some trees that grow by the side of 'holy' wells are known as prayer trees or rag trees in Ireland. Offerings of pieces of cloth are tied to the branches of these trees by people who visit the well hoping for cures for particular maladies. At Paphos in Cyprus there is a terebinth tree that is constantly festooned with fragments of cloth, including many handkerchiefs; I wonder if the people who left these are hoping to be cured of a common cold or a broken heart?

There are many countries where trees are hung with rags in this way; in Ireland, where the ancient thorn cult is slow to disappear, there used to be an old thorn growing by a well near Tinahely, County Wicklow. This tree was visited on 4 May every year by pilgrims who would circle the well and pray for a cure for their ailments. Pieces of material, torn from their clothes, were then hung on the thorn tree. Maybe the theory was that, as the cloth rotted away, the illness for which the pilgrim sought a cure would also fade. I hope so.

The spiritual and temporal power of Irish chieftains is thought to have been closely related to sacred trees, and because of this the home of the chief was always situated close to one of them. Rival chieftains, making a take-over bid for the territory, would mark out the sacred tree and fix it as their prime target; its destruction would symbolize the submission of the conquered tribe.

Nowadays we take Christmas trees into our homes, to stand in pride of place, decorated and admired at the dark time of the year. There is a great deal of lore telling of the sacred nature of trees, of the mystical bonds between trees and men and of the tree as a symbol of life, of inexhaustible fertility and of reality. Maybe that is also why we all have a family 'tree'.

Holly was frequently hung in dwelling places in the winter. As I mention in the section on 'Seeing Red' (page 19), the bright red colour of the berries was believed to have magical properties. The plant itself was said to shelter the spirit of the woods during the winter months, and taking a bough indoors protected the home and its inmates from witchcraft and lightning. This is one of many examples of pre-Christian practices becoming part of our Christmas celebrations. In fact, the prickles on holly leaves probably protect them from being eaten by goats, deer, ponies and cattle: if you look at a tall holly tree, you will see that only those leaves near the bottom of the tree are very prickly. Those nearer the top, which the animals cannot reach, have smoother edges.

TREE BARK, TO COVER AND PROTECT

Bark is the skin of the tree; it is a mass of dead, corky tissue which protects the layer of living cells, called the phloem, within the plant. The phloem is part of the vital vascular tissue which transports carbo-hydrates, manufactured in the leaves, to the roots and other parts of the plant. In southern Europe several species of pine are tapped for their resin; certain wines are flavoured with resin from the Aleppo pine. The phloem of the sugar maple is tapped for maple syrup. Maples used to be an important food source for native Americans who used maple sugar as their main sweetening agent. If a mature maple tree is tapped in early spring, before its leaves open, it can provide up to 144 litres (32 gallons) of sap. This is enough to produce 4$\frac{1}{2}$ litres (1 gallon) of syrup or more than 2 kg (about 5 lb) of sugar.

According to Christian tradition, when Jesus was born in Bethlehem, three wise men travelled from the east to bring Him gifts. One gift was of gold; but the other two were frankincense and myrrh, aromatic resins which were held in great esteem in those days. Frankincense comes from *Boswellia carteri*, a tree of lush growth, while myrrh is collected from a stunted, thorny tree of arid desert regions, called Commiphora myrrh. Both trees belong to the family Burseraceae, but their main similarity is that all parts of the plants contain resin, which exudes from ducts in the trunks of the trees, where it solidifies into tear-shaped drops.

So it is no wonder that in winter when food sources are scarce deer, rabbits and squirrels may eat away the bark of a tree to reach the nourishing phloem layer. If the animals damage the tree all round its trunk in this way, the tree will die; this is called ring barking.

The bark of a tree is its first line of defence; it is a guard in fire resistance, a shield against sudden changes in temperature and a protection from disease-bearing pathogens and from insect activity. The bark of some trees contains substances such as alkaloids and tannins which probably act as a preservative. The tannin from oak bark is used in tanning hides for leather.

But although bark protects the tree as best it can, the outside often splits and forms the familiar furrows that run up and down tree trunks. Deep fissures and cracks in bark shelter many overwintering invertebrates; centipedes, millipedes, woodlice, spiders and insects all find homes in the damp, sheltering darkness. These invertebrates are hunted by woodpeckers, nuthatches and treecreepers, birds which are easier to see during the winter months because of lack of foliage.

BIRDS ON THE BARK

Woodpeckers, nuthatches and treecreepers, the birds which find their food on tree trunks, are highly adapted climbers. They cling vertically and use their tails as a prop; only birds which forage regularly on tree trunks have stiffened tail feathers,

holly, ivy and mistletoe

sometimes with the tips of the two central veins missing to leave a spike, which acts as a grip on the bark.

Woodpeckers, in particular, rely on the two central tail feathers for support and delay shedding them when they moult until the replacement feathers have grown. It is essential to have a strong grip when chiselling into bark or poking into crevices to extricate some choice invertebrate; so the birds which are seen on tree bark have sharp, curved claws and powerful thigh muscles. Woodpeckers have two toes facing forward and two behind to give maximum grip; this arrangement is quite unusual in birds.

The 'tree-climbing' birds progress up and down trunks and along branches by pressing their tail down firmly and hopping. The usual pattern of the search for food is to hop up the trunk of one tree and then fly to the base of the next, but nuthatches are able to move upwards and horizontally; they are also so often seen coming down a tree head first that it was once commonly thought that they even roosted upside down!

Woodpeckers chisel into wood to search for insect larvae, woodlice and other invertebrates which hide behind loose bark or in the timber. A woodpecker's skull is especially thick-walled to absorb the impact of the striking hammer blows; and an amazingly long tongue probes the chiselled holes to reach the wood-boring grubs within.

The nuthatch wedges nuts into crevices in a tree, a post or a wall to hold them steady for hammering open; while the treecreeper's long, slender, finely pointed beak delicately picks tiny items of food from their hiding places in the fissures of bark.

The treecreeper is so well camouflaged that the first time I ever spotted one in its winter roost it made me jump. It was in an oval cavity, about the size of a hen's egg, in a tree trunk. It had snuggled vertically into the hollow with its back to the world and all its feathers fluffed out for maximum warmth.

AUTUMNAL BOUNTY

The word 'fruit' conjures up the image of a bowl of shining, succulent apples and oranges, but in botanical terms a fruit is the ripened ovary of any flowering plant, and contains the seeds. There are fleshy fruits and dry fruits; both categories are edible to an animal living in the wild, but fleshy fruits are to be eaten as they ripen, whereas dry fruits can be stored as insurance against a time when other food is scarce.

In autumn, along the hedgerows and in the woods,

treecreeper

plums, sloes, cherries, apples and blackberries offer a juicy feast to insects, birds and mammals – including human beings – while elderberries hang in profusion, to be gobbled up by flocks of nomadic starlings. Scarlet holly berries shine against the sky and bright, swollen hawthorn berries and rosehips glow as though their yellow flesh would burst through their glistening skins. The fruits of holly, hawthorn and rose are more durable than fleshy fruits, and can be left on the trees until winter has closed in and they are softened by the first frosts.

All fleshy fruits are adapted to being eaten by animals, as a means of ensuring that the seeds inside the fruits are dispersed. Once eaten, the fleshy part of the fruit is digested, but the seeds have a protective coat; they pass through the animal and are voided. These seeds are left to grow, in their own pile of dung, well away from the parent plant. Some plant species have become so well adapted to this method of seed dispersal that the seeds will only germinate if they have been acted upon by enzymes in an animal's digestive tract.

The seeds of dried fruits, on the other hand, are destroyed if they are eaten. Nuts rely on the safety of numbers. Most are eaten, but some are stored for

nuthatch

later in the winter by squirrels, mice or jays which do not always remember where they have hidden their cache; by then the nuts have been successfully dispersed and they begin to germinate in the spring. Beech mast, hazelnuts, chestnuts and acorns are among the fruits dispersed in this way. ('Mast' is an Anglo-Saxon word for meat, which we now only apply to the fruits of certain trees.)

There are other ways of ensuring that seeds are dispersed and grow a healthy distance from their parent plant. The dry fruits of the silver birch, ash, Scots pine and trees in the maple family have wings which enable the fruits to spin in the air like the rotor blade of a helicopter or glide away from the tree even on a still day. Some of these structures show considerable aerodynamic ability and pioneer aircraft designers studied the flight of these fruits intensively.

The seeds of dandelions, thistles, goat's beard and the willow herbs have tufts of silky hairs which make up a parachute, enabling the seeds to float in the wind. Goldfinches and other seed-eating birds feed avidly on thistle heads and help to disperse the floating seeds.

Some fruits are not attractive to animals as food; these may hitch a ride on the fur or feathers of any creature brushing past the plant. Enchanter's nightshade, cleavers and spotted medick have fruits with numerous tiny hooks which cling tightly – a method which the makers of the 'Velcro' fastener have found to be very efficient.

The seeds that are dispersed in their many ways in autumn pass through a stage of suspended activity or dormancy during the winter months. Some hard-coated seeds need a long cold period and will not germinate until they have been exposed to low temperatures. Gardeners will know that the seeds of some primulas, meconopsis and alpine plants have to be placed in a refrigerator for a few weeks before successful germination can take place; this cold treatment imitates the winter conditions that the seeds would have experienced in their natural habitat.

NATURAL NUTCRACKERS

The hawfinch has a large triangular beak which is silvery blue in summer, fading to yellow in late autumn and winter. The bird eats beech mast and the soft seeds of elm and hornbeam, but the beak has been developed to crack the stones of cherry, damson, plum, sloe and olive. It has four rounded knobs, two on each side of the lower mandible; placing the stone between these knobs means that the force for cracking is shared equally by muscles on either side of the head, allowing the bird to operate a crushing force of between 25 and 45 kg (60–95 lb). Hawthorn berries, rosehips and holly berries all form part of the hawfinch's diet, while its taste for green peas has made some enemies among gardeners and farmers. These very shy birds leave their woodland hide-outs in winter and form small feeding flocks, moving from place to place in open countryside.

In the finch family there is a wide range of bill shapes to suit a variety of diets. The crossbill is a specialist. It resembles a miniature parrot with its large head and beak. The males are brick red with a brown tail while the females, which have to be camouflaged when sitting on the nest, have a yellow-green plumage. Conifer seeds are the bird's principal food, although fruits and insects are taken from time to time. The crossbill pushes its partly opened beak behind a cone scale, gives a sharp sideways movement of the lower mandible and, with a jerk of the head, raises the scale and splits it. It then works the cone seed free with its tongue.

Members of the crow and tit families hold down cones, nuts and other hard seeds with one foot while hammering at them with the beak until the shell cracks.

The nutcracker of southern Scandinavia has a groove on its lower mandible and splits the shells of its favourite hazelnuts by fitting the nut into the groove and squeezing. The shell cracks as though in a nut-cracker. Nutcrackers bury stores of pine seeds, not only for their own winter food, but also to feed their young. Seeds are buried in late summer and autumn, and the birds seem to remember the position of their caches – they can locate them even under snow. They bury many more seeds than they need to survive, so helping to disperse the seeds of the tree on which they depend.

SEEING RED

I have been interested in the colour red for a long time, because of its power to attract and repel, to be dangerous – as in 'red for danger' – yet, according to folklore and among some animals, to have protective properties.

The hard red forewings of some ladybirds warn would-be predators that the ladybird tastes nasty; young, inexperienced predators often try to eat these attractively coloured insects, but find them so bitter that they spit them out and avoid them in future. So the ladybird's red colouring warns the predator of danger and protects the useful insect.

The male three-spined stickleback has a red breast during the breeding season. This warns other male sticklebacks to keep away from his territory, while attracting females to come into the area of his nest. The robin's red breast is used to good effect when another robin enters his territory; the defending robin pushes out his breast to make it conspicuous and fluffs out all his other feathers too so that he looks as big as possible. When an unattached female robin comes along in spring the male, who has defended his territory against all comers throughout the winter, behaves in exactly the same way to the female as he did to any other intruder; but the female is

fly agaric

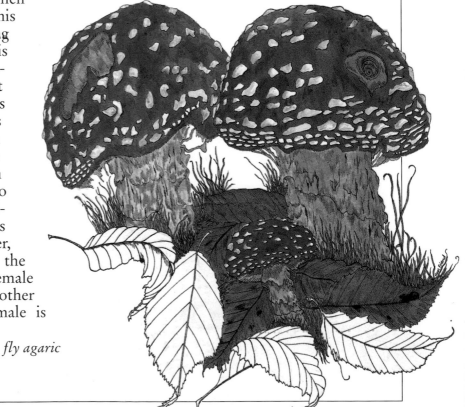

attracted by the expanse of red breast and stands her ground, singing back to her intended mate. After a day or two of sparring, she is accepted.

Some of the red fruits we see in the hedgerow are poisonous and we do well to be cautious about eating some of them. White bryony and black bryony – *Bryonia dioica* and *Tamus communis* – have red globular fruits which, if eaten in quantity, make a person very ill. The red pendulous fruits of the woody nightshade, *Solanum dulcamara*, slow down the heart rate and lower both blood pressure and body temperature. Lords and ladies and cuckoo pint, *Arum italicum* and *Arum maculatum*, have orange-scarlet berries which can make one feel quite unwell; while the orange-red seeds of stinking iris, *Iris foetidissima*, contain a poison which is a severe irritant on the alimentary tract. But the red fruits of holly, rowan, hawthorn, rose, cherry, tomato, apple and raspberry are perfectly edible, and the red colour seems to be a signal to the birds to come and eat.

Under the birch trees, among the fallen leaves, fly agaric fungi, *Amanita muscaria*, spread their red caps flecked with white. This fungus is so called because it contains toxins which can stun and kill flies. It is just one of a number of fungi which induce hallucinations when eaten; it is not advisable to try them, as serious physical damage may result. But fly agaric was probably used in the ceremonials of ancient religions to induce ritual hallucinations.

So, red can warn of danger, but at the same time it can be an attractant. Can it be that our ancestors used the attractant/repellent forces of the colour as a sort of lightning conductor, a tangible object that attracts danger and carries it safely away? At the dark time of the year they took in boughs bearing red berries because they believed that the magical colour red would protect them, their animals and their homes from all manner of evils. The belief must have been very strong as it has survived to the present day. The use of red cloth to counteract or enhance magic, or ward off the evil eye, is widespread; in the East, red clothes and decorations are regarded as auspicious and are worn at weddings and other joyful occasions. Hindu women wear a small, red, circular spot on their forehead, called a 'tikka'. Women displaying this symbol are in a happy state, a state of blessedness and the tikka is worn for good fortune; for this reason, widows and women in mourning do not wear it. Meanwhile, many of us continue to decorate our homes with red ribbons, red-berried holly and red paper chains at Christmas time. I wonder why?

●

KEEPING THE COLD AT BAY

The surrounding air temperature is of extreme importance to animals as it controls the speed of chemical reactions in the body. These reactions provide the animal with energy, so the amount of energy available to be drawn on depends on the outside temperature.

Fish, reptiles, amphibians and all invertebrates are called cold-blooded because they are unable to control their own body heat and so their bodies take on the temperature of the surrounding air or water. In fact 'cold-blooded' is not a very accurate description; the proper term is 'poikilothermic', which means 'of *variable* temperature'. Many so-called cold-blooded creatures bask in the sun and absorb a good deal of heat radiating out of the ground. In very hot conditions the chemical reactions of these animals are so fast that the animal becomes exhausted, but when the surrounding temperature is too cold, the reactions are so slow that the animal can hardly function.

A friend of mine who is in the book trade experienced this first hand when she wanted to use a live scorpion in a photograph for a book jacket. (The book was about buried treasures and it was thought that scorpion tracks in the sand would be a nice touch, suggestive of danger and exoticism.) The scorpion was delivered the day before the photographic session and the question arose as to what would be the safest way to store this far from cuddly guest. The handler advised her to keep it in a box in the fridge overnight. The cold would slow down its metabolism sufficiently to render it safe and make an escape attempt unlikely.

Birds and mammals are warm-blooded; they escape these problems because they have ways of keeping their body temperature at more or less the same level despite the surrounding air temperature. To do this they have to be able to store heat when the weather is cold and lose it on a hot day. Fur and feathers are good insulators which keep the body warm in cold climates, and prevent too much heat

hips and haws

entering in hot conditions. In order to cool the body down animals sweat, so releasing water vapour which evaporates and cools the skin.

Some animals, finding the weather very cold, form an aggregation – a group of animals that gather together in response to a particular environmental factor. Birds such as redwings and fieldfares form feeding flocks, banding together to fly from one food source to the next throughout the months of hardship, roosting in thickets to keep warm at night. I once counted more than twenty wrens going into a modestly sized nest-box on a cold winter's evening. The number amazed me, but I am assured that up to forty of these tiny birds will huddle together in a feathery bundle, each one warming its neighbour.

FUR . . .

A mammal's coat is made up of two kinds of hair. The outside layer is composed of guard hairs which are waterproofed by oil secretions from special glands known as sebaceous glands. The guard hairs protect the short, soft underfur; this traps air among its many strands and helps to keep the animal warm. The insulating power of fur depends on the amount of air, which is a poor conductor of heat, that is trapped within the coat. The thickness of an animal's fur coat varies according to the season: winter fur is dense in order to trap as much warm air as possible around the body. Some mammals moult their fur twice a year, in spring and in autumn. For example, the field vole moults some of its old coat in autumn, but gains extra fur as more hairs grow in their place; these are extra fine and act as good insulation. Other small mammals, including the field mouse and shrew, also undergo this sort of coat change in autumn.

The structure of deer hair is different to that of most other animal hair in that each hair contains larger hair spaces; so because of their increased thickness the winter hairs are packed closer together. Reindeer overwintering in Finland, Norway, the mountains of Sweden and the Cairngorms of Scotland are well adapted to severe winter weather conditions. The North American moose has a similarly insulated coat. Moose, by the way, are known as elk in Europe. The animals known as elk in North America are really wapiti, which are similar to the creature Europeans call the red deer. This can all be most confusing and is a good example of the need for 'official' zoological names.

The long, hollow hairs of the reindeer's outer coat cover a short, soft, woolly fur; a heat-exchange network of arteries and veins prevents the nose, legs and hooves from allowing the body heat to be lost through them to the atmosphere. The deeply cleft, splayed hooves are

The introduction of subspecies from different parts of the pheasant's natural range has led to great variety in the male's plumage.

adapted to long months spent on snow and soft ground; they act like snow shoes, spreading the weight of the reindeer and preventing it from sinking too far into snow or boggy terrain. These well-designed feet are able to scrape away deep snow so that the reindeer can get at lichens growing underneath. Reindeer graze on grasses, twigs, leaves and herbaceous plants in summer, but in winter they search for lichens, particularly the one called reindeer moss.

Sheep are rather different, as their wool is all composed of very long underfur without the protective outside layer of guard hairs; to compensate the wool is oily and this helps to keep out the rain. Wild sheep have seasonal moults, so that they are not too hot in summer, but domestic sheep have more or less lost the ability to moult and they have to be shorn in early summer. Their fleece grows thick again before winter returns. Walking the moors of the Peak District in Derbyshire, near my home, I often see sheep that have evaded the shearing: their fleece seems to peel back like an orange skin, helped free by brambles and barbed wire, revealing the downy pink skin beneath.

Many different breeds and cross-breeds of sheep live on lowlands and hills in countries such as Britain, New Zealand, Australia, Argentina and much of Europe. There are three main types: long-wools, shortwools and hill breeds. Longwools have long, shiny fleeces; they need rich land and good food in order to produce their wool, which is used to make smooth worsted cloth. Shortwools have short, curly fleeces, used to make woollen yarns suitable for knitwear; they are big, slow sheep with heavy coats. Among the most important of the shortwools are the Merinos; they belong to a breed that was developed in Spain and their fleeces are renowned worldwide as the basis of the wool industry. These sheep produce very fine wool, with long fibres and little tendency to shrink – factors of great importance. Merinos are very adaptable, so they can be kept in many different types of country; they are particularly popular in Australia.

Hills usually have short grass, so the most numerous sheep are the hill breeds, adapted to the colder and less predictable weather found in these situations. They were probably one of the first animals to be domesticated. Almost no climate is too inhospitable for these animals; they graze on the slopes of hills where the grass is thin, the wind bites, the rain drives down and the snow drifts. Sheep are able to forage through light snow to find grass and heather shoots on which to nibble. Most of them can rely on farmers bringing food for them during long spells of severe weather, but others have to manage as best they can. Only the fittest animals are able to cope with the combination of harsh climate and poor grazing. The fleeces of hill sheep are used for a variety of purposes: the coarsest for carpets, intermediate quality for tweeds and the finest for knitwear and flannel.

. . . AND FEATHERS

Like fur, feathers come in two main kinds: waterproof outer flight or contour feathers – called pennae – and inner down feathers.

A typical flight or contour feather has a central shaft, or quill, which is hollow at its base, and a vane which is composed of rows of barbs. Each barb is virtually a miniature feather carrying several hundred tiny barbules with minute hooks which latch into the barbules from the barb above them. This fastening system is so efficient that if two barbs are separated and the vane of the feather is split, the bird has only to draw the feather through the tips of its beak once or twice, 'nibbling' from the feather base outwards, to restore the vane to its immaculate state. You can see this happen if you ruffle a feather, then restore it to shape by running it between your fingers.

There is often a secondary feather at the base of the contour feather; it is usually small and downy and forms an extra layer of insulation against heat loss. Down feathers are fluffy because they have no hooks on their barbules; their main purpose is heat preservation.

Birds have many more feathers in winter than in summer, suggesting that insulation as well as flight was a major factor in their evolution. When a bird fluffs its feathers up in cold weather, it is thickening the blanket of warm air between the outer and inner layers of feathers. Birds need effective insulation from the cold, as they must maintain a body temperature of about 41°C (106°F) – this is very hot in human terms. In severe winters when food is scarce, even feathers cannot prevent birds from freezing to death.

Only penguins are able to survive in winter on the Antarctic ice-cap, the coldest place on earth. These birds, symbolic of the frozen south, probably originated in the milder parts of the southern hemisphere where some species live today – in the warm waters of the Galapagos, southern Africa and south Australia. But the penguins of the Antarctic swim in icy waters, walk long distances over sea ice, withstand blizzards and stand for weeks on end in temperatures of forty degrees below zero. Obviously, they need extremely effective insulation to enable them to endure this sort of terrible cold, and their feathers have developed to provide this.

Penguin feathers are long and narrow, with tips that turn in

crossbills

towards the body. The shaft of each feather has a fluffy tuft at the base; these tufts mat together and form a layer very like fur that covers the penguin's body uniformly and is practically impenetrable to wind and water. When penguins moult, the new feathers grow into the old ones; only when this has happened does the penguin comb off the old feathers, so renewing its entire plumage without being exposed to the perils of cold air or sea.

Birds have to take great care of their feathers; they wash them in water, ruffle them in dust and service them regularly in order to maintain their flying and waterproofing efficiency. Birds of both fresh water and the sea are at great risk from the results of human thoughtlessness, lack of care and, sometimes, bad intentions. Chemical outlets from industry, sewage and rubbish from cities, on coasts and rivers, oil spillage from giant tankers and drilling sites are only a few examples of the ways in which we are polluting the waters we share with other animals. Oil, chemicals, excess fertilizers and the run-off from rubbish harm animals directly; they also enter the food chain, slowly poisoning animals or rendering them sterile. Oil-smeared feathers and fur lead to death, too. Even small amounts of oil may prove lethal by ruining the insulating properties of plumage and pelage, but when animals are covered in oil they stand very little chance of survival. Oil smoothes water surfaces, luring birds to settle on them and then polluting their feathers; when a ship releases an oil slick that drifts towards the shore, coastal birds find it difficult to escape. Mammals such as seals, otters, dolphins and porpoises suffer or die when oil is spilt at sea. Unfortunately, the detergents that are often used to break up oil slicks contain toxic ingredients that are as harmful to birds and marine life as the oil itself. When oil tankers are involved in accidents at sea the result is an ecological disaster affecting all marine life in the area, be it plant or microscopic animal.

Most birds oil their plumage by anointing each individual feather with a secretion from their preen gland – the so-called parson's nose – which is situated in the tail area. This grooming cleans the feathers and leaves them supple and water-resistant. When the oil from the preen gland is ingested, it supplies the bird with an added form of Vitamin D called calciferol; this is also synthesized in the skin under the influence of sunlight. Vitamin D promotes the absorption of calcium and phosphate by the gut and their uptake into the bones. A bird cannot, of course, preen its own head; instead it transfers oil from the beak to a foot and scratches the head with that foot while balancing on the other. A few birds, including the cormorant and gannet, have a special claw with 'teeth' like a comb on the inside edge of the third toe; this is used to scratch the feathers of the head and neck and so keep them in good order.

Some birds, such as herons, pigeons and parrots, do not have a preen gland. Instead they have modified body feathers which grow continuously and then break down into a talcum powder-like substance which permeates the feathers when the birds preen.

Feathers wear out or are lost by accident, so they have to be replaced; but the entire plumage is replaced at regular intervals, usually yearly. Old feathers are pushed out by new ones, which grow from the same follicles; it takes an average-sized bird such as a blackbird three or four months to replace its old feathers with new ones. The new feathers of most birds are replaced in sequence and in pairs from either side of the body, although there are many variations. Usually the primary or large flight feathers at the wing-ends are the first to be changed. These are followed by the secondaries, the wing feathers nearer to the body which give the bird 'lift' and keep it in the air. Tail feathers are shed in several ways: songbirds, for example, shed them in pairs from the central pair outwards; body feathers are then shed.

As you can imagine, the moulting of wing feathers restricts the birds' flying ability and some find a retreat where they can feel safe until their new wing feathers are in place. Many water birds, such as swans, geese and ducks, shed all their flight feathers at once and are unable to fly for weeks, making them very vulnerable. To escape predators, they move to marshes, mud-flats, sheltered waters or dense vegetation where they can change their feathers in relative safety. So new feathers are usually grown when food is still plentiful, ensuring that the bird's plumage is in good condition when winter stretches out a cold hand.

CAMOUFLAGE DRESS

As the days become shorter, animals begin to grow thicker coats, and some change the colour of their fur or feathers from summer hues to winter white. Animals which become paler in winter live in areas where that season is hard and there is a strong likelihood of the ground being covered in snow, so camouflage is almost certainly one reason for the change.

Mountain, or blue, hares, which live at high altitudes and high latitudes, crouch in a shallow form or scrape amongst the heather or on a more open hillside. If they retained their grey-brown pelage in winter they might easily fall victim to passing birds of prey. In October, the lighter-weight male apparently begins to feel the cold first and starts to change to a white winter coat; the heavier female follows suit when she feels cold. First the furred hind feet become white, and gradually the colour change moves over the body, reaching the head last of all. Only the tips of the ears remain black. The hare does not moult its autumn coat until its winter coat is fully grown, so there is always protection from the cold; the white winter fur is thicker and longer than the autumn coat, and there is lots of underfur to keep out icy winds.

The Peak District, where I live, is the only place in England where mountain hares are to be found. They were introduced into this area from Scotland in the 1860s and soon found the high moorland to their liking, so the population increased. They are easy to see in snow-free conditions, but as soon as the first snow falls, they are almost perfectly camouflaged, crouching as still as can be in their form and only leaping away at the last minute to avoid being stepped on. During the short winter days they feed on heather and cotton grass, digging through the soft snow if necessary to reach the vegetation buried beneath it. However, if the snow becomes ice-crusted or is very deep, they are unable to dig down and have to look for juniper, willow or rowan twigs to nibble. When grazing, they keep their backs to the wind and feed in a half circle, moving slowly forwards about 30 cm (1 ft) at a time. During storms, mountain hares gather into larger groups on the sheltered side of ridges, making scrapes in the snow for shelter. Many die of starvation in prolonged, severe winters.

Mountain hares can be found in Ireland, Scotland, northern parts of Europe and Asia, and in the Alps. In Alaska, Canada and mountainous regions of the continental United States there is a similar creature called the snowshoe, which changes from summer brown to winter buff, a colour that undoubtedly has camouflage value.

Stoats are widespread in the northern hemisphere. In the southern parts of their range, they keep their chestnut-brown colouring throughout the year. Those living further north may become paler in winter, but the stoats of the far north change their coat to that of ermine – white with a black tail-tip – which gives them camouflage when they stalk their prey. The stoat is a fierce animal with little to fear from predators – although adults are occasionally taken by larger mammals, hawks and owls, so the white pelage may act in a defensive way, too. Both red and grey squirrels have paler coats in winter, and deer moult to a more subdued shade of brown for the winter period.

The Arctic regions of Europe, Asia and North America have short summers, when lichens, mosses and many flowering plants flourish on the tundra and provide food for herbivores. During the long, cold, winter months, ice and snow cover much of the land and there are few animals to be seen. However, surviving on these frozen wastes are three mammals which change the colour of their fur to camouflage themselves – the lemming, the Arctic fox and the Arctic hare.

Mountain hares are well camouflaged on desolate moorland,
where they crouch in scrapes on the open ground.

Lemmings are preyed on by the Arctic fox and the snowy owl, so they try to keep a low profile by travelling about along runways close to the ground, beneath the snow. It is much warmer under the snow than out in the open, and these small, fat, guinea pig-like rodents trot along their snow-topped corridors nibbling the vegetation. When an Arctic fox becomes aware of their presence, it pounces, stiff-legged, trying to force the lemmings out of their tunnels; or it digs deep into the snow in an attempt to scoop its prey out.

While the Arctic fox is hunting in this way, it is often watched by a snowy owl which, seeing the fox catch a lemming, will fly down and try to drive it away from the kill. Lemmings form a major part of the diet of the Arctic fox and the snowy owl; so much so, that the numbers of the predators fluctuate with the availability of lemmings.

The Arctic fox is a rounder, sturdier animal than the red fox. Its nose is less pointed and its ears are shorter and more rounded; these are adaptations to reduce the risk of frostbite in the intense cold. The Arctic fox is able to withstand temperatures as low as –50°C (–58°F). During the short summer, it is greyish brown in colour, and this changes to a creamy white as winter approaches. Like the red fox, the Arctic fox is flexible in its behaviour, travelling long distances to find food and hunting by day or by night. Any food that can't be eaten at once is stored in a hole in the snow, or in a crevice of rock.

Arctic foxes also hunt for Arctic hares, which are camouflaged in winter-white fur. These hares have great difficulty in finding food when snow covers the tundra; they must dig deep into the snow in an attempt to find leaves to keep them from starving. The few leaves that the hares find are tough and, although they supplement these with lichen nibbled from rocks, it is a poor diet in the freezing temperatures. All the time the hares are searching for food they must watch out for predators and they sometimes gather in large groups, probably because there is safety in numbers: with any luck, at least one pair of eyes will see the approach of danger and warn the others. In these conditions only the fittest animals are able to survive.

Many birds face a conflict between the need to blend in with their habitat and the instinct to advertise themselves to others of their kind when defending a territory or during courtship. Some species – kingfishers, for example – are known to be distasteful to predators, so are able to wear brightly coloured feathers. Most others have to achieve a compromise. Many do this by discarding their worn summer plumage at the end of the breeding season, to have it replaced by a winter plumage of a different colour. Wading birds such as turnstones, knot

Arctic lemmings feed in the 'corridors' between the ground and the snow layer, beneath the feet of their major predators.

and dunlin have dull plumage when they overwinter on the seashore, but by the time they migrate northwards to breed they have moulted to brighter colours. Turnstones breed in Scandinavia, Greenland and Canada; knots fly to Siberia, Greenland and north-eastern Canada to nest; dunlins breed in Siberia, Scandinavia, Iceland, Greenland and the north of Scotland.

The ptarmigan, a bird of high barren mountains, hides from its enemies by changing its colour with the seasons, so becoming an inconspicuous part of the landscape all year round. In summer it is brown, mottled with black; only the wings and underparts are white. Gradually the feathers change, so that in autumn the upper parts, breast and flanks are grey-brown mottled with white. In winter the ptarmigan is white, with a dark brown tail and eye stripe.

The red grouse lives in northern and western Britain and in Scandinavia – where it is called the willow grouse. There are two distinct races: the red grouse of the British Isles remains a mottled dark brown throughout the year, while the willow grouse of Scandinavia has white wings and belly in the summer and becomes all white – apart from the dark tail – in winter. The ptarmigan, the red grouse and the willow grouse all have white feathers on their legs and toes, so as to reduce heat loss during the long winters spent crouching or burrowing into the snow for shelter and searching for seeds, fruits, leaves and shoots beneath it.

These birds live on the nutritious shoots of heathers, bilberry and crowberry (*Empetrum nigrum*). This food is particularly important during the period when the female is developing her eggs; it has been found that if the hen eats well before she lays, the subsequent chicks will

stoat

have a better chance of surviving their first crucial weeks of life. As food quality is of the greatest importance to successful breeding, the territory won by the male must be one with plenty of healthy food plants. The territory of a grouse or ptarmigan need only be small if the food supply is good, but the gaining of it is vital for males; not only because it allows them to breed, but also because it helps them prolong their own survival. Males without territories are driven away by more successful rivals and are doomed to starvation and predation.

Colour change is very important in predatory behaviour, as predators need to be sure that they are not noticed by their prey; by the same token, it is an advantage for an animal to be able to merge into the background in order to avoid becoming a victim. The polar bear's fur is always creamy white as the animal spends both its summers and its winters on snow or ice floes. The concealment given by its white coat enables the polar bear to stalk the seals on which it lives, so its camouflage is offensive. There is no defensive advantage to the bear as it does not have predators which hunt it for food. The only danger to this animal is from the guns of hunters who shoot it for the sake of its fur. It is therefore ironical – but true – that this form of adaptation to environment came about as a way of ensuring winter survival.

robin

WINTER WEATHER

Winter is a time of short days and long, cold hours of darkness; a time when, in nature, the processes of life continue, but at a much slower pace. This is a harsh time of year when there may be snow falls, heavy rain, high winds, fog or frost, all mixed in with the occasional sunny day to raise our spirits before the next quirk in the weather pattern comes along to try us once more.

REPEATING PATTERNS

From the time of early man, humans have celebrated the change of the seasons, marvelled at the atmospheric lights in the rainbow and in the aurora borealis – the northern lights – or the aurora australis – the southern lights – and have been awestruck at the power of hurricanes and tornadoes. We now understand the causes of these phenomena better, but they still retain some of their mystery.

All events that happen in nature involve time cycles, and these cycles are governed by the turning of the earth. We say that the sun rises in the east and sinks in the west, because the sun appears to move across the sky during the day. However, this is inaccurate – it is really the earth that is moving.

Gravitational forces have moulded the earth into a spherical shape that bulges slightly at the equator. Imagine a line running through the earth from the North to the South Pole; this line is the earth's axis. Every twenty-four hours the earth turns once on its axis; each part of the world passes through the sun's light, which gives day, and the sun's shadow, which is night. Not only does the earth turn on its axis, it also travels round the sun once every 365 days 5 hours 48 minutes and 46 seconds. As the earth rotates on its axis and slowly moves around the sun, it tilts to one side, so that first one hemisphere and then the other leans towards the sun. When the northern hemisphere tilts towards the sun, we in northern latitudes receive more daylight and heat. This is summer, and the longest day, or summer solstice, is on 21 June. When

Trees take on a distinctive character once their leaves have fallen and the details of their branching pattern can be seen.

the northern hemisphere tilts away from the sun, we receive less day-light and heat. This is winter; the shortest day, or winter solstice, is on 22 December. Twice a year there are times when neither hemisphere points towards the sun and at these times day and night are exactly equal in length. These are the equinoxes; the vernal, or spring, equinox is on 20 or 21 March and the autumnal equinox is on 22 or 23 September.

The change of seasons has a profound effect on all aspects of the lives of plants and animals. The seasons gradually change as the days become longer and warmer, or shorter and cooler. Plants and animals are sensitive to the length of day and night; they respond to an unseen biological clock, measuring the daylight or darkness as though looking at a watch. Flowers open in the morning and close at night according to an approximately twenty-four-hour cycle known as the circadian, or diurnal, rhythm. The same pattern can be seen in the sleeping and waking hours of animals. If you have a dog or cat you will have noticed how it divides the day into periods of sleep and periods of activity. Humans, too, have circadian rhythms. Even in the northern-most latitudes where the sun never rises during the midwinter months, the normal rhythm of sleep and activity persists.

Perhaps a better known aspect of biological timing is the fact that plants flower, and animals breed, at specific times of the year. The ability of an organism to measure the length of the day and to set its reproductive and other developmental functions by the amount of daylight it receives is called photoperiodism.

There are many examples of annual rhythms which you will have seen in action, and you can watch out for them year after year. These include the courtship, nest-building and migration of birds; the appearance of butterflies in the garden; the reproduction and hiberna-tion of mammals and other animals; and the germination, growth, flowering and leaf fall of plants. The physiological basis of these rhythms varies, but they are usually brought about by the seasonal change of temperature and/or day length.

It is very easy to take this annual rhythm of plant growth for granted; indeed, the effect of day or night length was not investigated until the beginning of this century. Now horticulturalists use their knowledge of photoperiodism when growing crops for market; by giving vegetable crops protection, warmth and artificial light, growers are able to sell their produce all year round. For example, lettuce, by nature a long-day/short-night plant, used only to be available during the long days of summer – we are now able to buy it throughout the year. Flowers, too, are 'tricked' into flowering at other times of the year than their seasonal norm, and the cut flower trade benefits from the ability of growers to adjust the day length according to the crop. Using artificial light to increase the day length will induce long-day plants to flower during short daylight hours. Short-day plants, such as mid-season and early-flowering chrysanthemums, can have their flowering times delayed if a day length of over fourteen and a half hours is provided from mid-August to mid-October. Conversely, using black-out screens to shorten the day means that other short-day plants can be induced to flower during the summer months.

It has been discovered that a single flash of light during the dark period cancels out the effect of a long night. The plants subjected to such treatment will behave as though they had not had a long night, making it easier for growers to produce long-day/short-night plants throughout the winter.

You can experiment with day length using the popular short-day/long-night houseplant poinsettia, *Euphorbia pulcherrima*. This produces beautiful red bracts during the winter months and adorns many homes at Christmas time. But as the days grow longer the bracts fall, and a surprising number of people throw their plant away; others feed it through the summer and are disappointed when the red bracts do not reappear the following autumn, although the plant seems healthy enough. Instead of putting your poinsettia on the compost heap in spring, you can continue to care for it by allowing it plenty of light and keeping the soil damp, but not wet. At the beginning of October you must begin to subject the poinsettia to photoperiodic

winter aconite

treatment, or it will not present the red bracts. Put it somewhere where it will have fourteen consecutive hours of darkness every day – in a warm, dark cupboard, or in a cardboard box in a warm room, from six o'clock in the evening until eight in the morning. Return it to its usual light position during the day. By December the bracts will have coloured and you will be able to display your plant in the usual way.

There are some cases where the annual rhythm depends on the lunar cycle. During the first three days of the third quarter of the moon in October and again at the same time in November, the palolo worms of the southern Pacific Ocean breed. It is not known how these reef-dwelling worms synchronize their timing, for the moon's third quarter occurs ten or eleven days earlier each year, until it slips back a month. Nevertheless, whether the sky is clear or overcast, at dawn, at this phase of the moon, the worms mate.

Palolo worms have a way of mating which brings egg and sperm together without the animals having to leave their safe, solitary tunnels to face a hazardous journey to the surface of the sea. Each worm is either male or female and has a 30 cm (1 ft) long segmented body, like an earthworm. The sex glands develop on the rear half of the worm. When the time for breeding arrives, each worm projects the end of its body out of its tunnel and breaks it off. All the many 'tails' wriggle towards the light at the surface, where the thin skins rupture in the waves and sperm and eggs are released, to fertilize and be fertilized at random. Many of these tails are eaten by predators, including the people of Samoa and Fiji, but the adult worms continue nibbling the coral polyps inside their burrows where they remain undisturbed. Their offspring join the zooplankton while they are developing; then when they mature they find a hole of their own and the cycle begins again.

WEATHER SOURCES

The science of the atmosphere and its phenomena is called meteorology. Weather is the state of the atmosphere over a particular region at a given moment; whereas climate indicates the characteristic features of the weather in that region over a period of time. I suppose the unpredictable nature of the weather adds a bit of spice to life; it is certainly something to begin conversations with, being an interest we all have in common.

The key force in determining weather is the

poinsettia

sun. The sun warms the earth unevenly, with the equatorial regions receiving more light and heat than the polar regions; when the sun heats the tropics, the air, warmed by convection currents, moves towards the poles. As this happens, the cold air of the Arctic and Antarctic regions is sucked towards the equator. The flow of air travelling to and from the tropics is affected by the rotation of the earth beneath; so the wind turns west to east in the northern hemisphere and east to west in the southern hemisphere. This is known as the Coriolis effect, a force which also acts on oceanic currents. If the earth was smooth, like a ball, and covered by sea or by a flat landmass, the air currents would be uniform and predictable and the weather unchanging. But the presence of landmasses with mountains, valleys, ice caps and deserts, together with the movements of the oceans, interfere with the flow of air currents, making the weather complex.

Land heats up and cools down quicker than water, so the land is hotter than the sea in summer and cooler than the sea in winter. By day cooler air from the sea moves in to replace the warm air that rises from the land; overnight and in the early morning there is a breeze from the land as air moves away from the cooler inland areas.

Water occurs in the atmosphere in the form of water vapour, liquid water and solid water – ice. Water vapour permeates the atmosphere and is largely responsible for the weather we experience from day to day. Almost all the atmospheric water vapour – along with most of the aerosols, both natural and manmade – hangs in suspension in the first layer of the atmosphere, the troposphere. This name comes from a Greek word meaning to turn or mix, and it is in the troposphere that most of the atmospheric turbulence and weather features occur.

Warm air holds more water vapour than cold air; thus as the air temperature increases, so does the amount of water vapour it can hold and the less likely this vapour is to fall as rain. One of the ways of predicting the probability of rain is to measure air pressure, which is defined as the weight of a column of air above a certain point. Many people have an aneroid barometer hanging in their home in order to watch its fluctuations. The instrument itself is fairly simple: it usually consists of a bank of hollow, circular, stainless steel discs called aneroids. The discs expand slightly when the air pressure falls and compress when it rises; one end of the bank of discs is attached to a rigid frame, while the other is connected to a needle which registers the air pressure. Surprisingly, damp air weighs less than dry air, so it exerts less pressure on the barometer. A steady high reading on a barometer indicates fair weather, while a rising barometer means clearing conditions and a falling one means that rain is on the way.

Cones open and close their woody scales according to the dampness in the atmosphere. This process is controlled by moisture-sensitive cells at the base of each scale: when the air is dry, the scales move apart; when it is damp, they close up. Cones need this ability to open and close their scales because, if the ripe cones on the tree were to open their scales in the rain, the seeds would simply fall to the ground under the parent tree and not be carried to a new place to grow. So the cones open when it is dry and the seeds have a much better chance of being scattered by a breeze.

Cones retain this ability to open and close their scales even when separated from their parent tree; as a result, some people use them as a sort of barometer, hanging them outside in the hope of foretelling the weather. This is an interesting phenomenon that you may like to observe, but it has one drawback – cone 'barometers' respond to changes in the weather only after they have happened!

There no longer seems to be a typical European weather pattern, but in those winters that we think of as 'normal' the following events usually occur. High pressure – an anticyclone – over continental Europe is overtaken every few days by a succession of low-pressure areas – depressions – which move in from the Atlantic. This results in clear, cold conditions over eastern and central Europe, and unsettled, cloudy and usually wet weather to the north and west. Sometimes, the high pressure regions move northwards and westwards, allowing cold, easterly airstreams to assail western Europe. Airstreams from this direction pass over very cold land and bring extremely wintry weather to northern France and south-eastern England in particular. Under these circumstances, the northern part of Britain suffers less, as the North Sea warms the air to a certain extent and so acts as a buffer.

Another warming influence is the ocean current known as the Gulf Stream, which develops from the Southern Equatorial Current in the Gulf of Mexico. The Gulf Stream then flows into the Straits of Florida. Travelling at a speed of 6.4 km (4 miles) an hour, it moves north along the east coast of the United States until it merges with another current called the North Atlantic Drift and veers north-eastwards across the Atlantic.

As the Gulf Stream nears Europe, it splits into two branches. One turns southwards and becomes the Canary Current, warming the seas off the west coasts of France, Spain, Portugal and North Africa; the other continues flowing northwards, bringing milder water to the seas around Ireland and off the west coasts of Britain and Norway as far north as Spitsbergen in the Arctic Ocean. When the Gulf Stream begins its journey it has a temperature of about 27°C (80°F), but as it makes its way northwards the temperature gradually falls. Nevertheless the slightly warmer waters – and the associated milder climate – attract migrant birds to the shores of the countries which it laps.

hedge maple and black bryony

RAIN, HAIL, SNOW AND FROST

The evaporation and condensation of water in the atmosphere are among the most important factors affecting the weather. One of the functions of air-conditioning systems, installed in many buildings, is to regulate the amount of moisture in the air, keeping it at a comfortable level at all times. Outside, of course, we are at the mercy of the ever-changing elements.

When moist air cools, the excess water vapour will condense into a fog of tiny, settling droplets. In certain circumstances, these droplets may remain liquid even at temperatures below their normal freezing point – they are then described as 'supercooled'. Should this take place in rising air currents at some distance above the ground, clouds are formed. Clouds contain huge numbers of supercooled water droplets and ice crystals, which begin to form when the cloud temperature is below −12°C (+10°F). The ice crystals grow at the expense of the water droplets, until they are big enough and heavy enough to fall. As a crystal falls it encounters progressively warmer air and, providing it has sufficient time to melt, it will reach the ground as rain. If it passes through 900 metres (3,000 ft) of air at a temperature above 0°C (32°F), it will melt; a shorter distance might give sleet, and if the ice crystals pass through only 300 metres (1,000 ft) of air, they will arrive as wet snow. Raindrops are formed when the water droplets coalesce. In the warm, dry conditions of a desert, raindrops may evaporate completely before they land; or evaporation may be so fast at ground level that the rain doesn't have a chance of seeping into the earth.

A rainbow appears when sunlight passes through the vast numbers of raindrops that are in the air during a shower. This phenomenon takes the form of an arc in the part of the sky opposite the sun, showing all the colours of the spectrum. A colourless beam of sunlight is called white light, but when it is refracted – that is, made to change direction – the rays spread out to show the bands of colour we see in a rainbow. The sun's rays are refracted when they enter a water droplet. They are reflected from the 'back' surface of the droplet, and then refracted again as they pass out through the 'front'. The light is dispersed in such a way that colours come through at slightly different angles, resulting in a rainbow. The colour and intensity of a rainbow depends on the size of the raindrops; larger drops produce brighter colours, dominated by red. Brilliant hues are also produced when sunlight passes through crystal and transparent gemstones.

We see a rainbow as seven colours – red, orange, yellow, green, blue, indigo and violet – but the spectrum really consists of an endless number of colours. The thing we recognize as a particular colour is really a specific wavelength of light. Colours travel at different speeds, though the variation in speed is very small. Paints or pigments absorb or sift out certain wavelengths from the white light falling on them, and reflect the rest. For example, a ripe tomato looks red in ordinary daylight, because the pigments in its skin absorb all other colours and reflect only the red wavelength. Plants containing chlorophyll absorb all the colours in the visible range with the exception of green light, which is reflected.

Colour adds to the interest and beauty of the world around us, and it has been found that the colours in our immediate surroundings have an emotional effect on our lives. People living in countries where snow dominates for much of the year often make up for the lack of colour in their environment by wearing bright clothes and producing colourful artifacts.

Hail forms in supercooled thunderclouds where water droplets merge and freeze. The irregular particles of ice – hailstones – fall to earth with great force, often causing damage. Large hailstones form when very strong storm currents circulate within the cloud for some time, moving between very cold high levels and relatively warm low levels. The core of each hailstone gathers layers, one of which is opaque and forms when the core collides with ice crystals and small supercooled droplets near the cloud tops. The enlarging hailstones gather a clear ice coating when they collide with the bigger droplets near the cloud base. Each round trip that the hailstones make within the thundercloud gives them extra layers and they become bigger and bigger. Some people insist that they have seen hailstones as big as golf balls. I wonder!

The icy crystals that become snowflakes form around minute, floating dust or salt particles. When water droplets freeze, crystals of various shapes, such as needles, prisms, stars and plates, are formed. The crystals have a diameter ranging from 0.01 mm to a few millimetres and a thickness of about a

ice crystals

43

thousandth of their diameter. Each is a symmetrical hexagon, and every one is distinct, differing in size, design and surface markings; this is remarkable when you consider the numbers of snowflakes that fall during a snowstorm! When snow accumulates on the ground, it is a good insulator of sound and warmth. The layer nearest to the earth is the warmest, as it traps the heat beneath it and reflects any sunlight that hits it from above. This means that plants with green leaves, trapped underneath the snow, are not exposed to frost and so are able to survive. Small herbivores such as mice and voles take advantage of this by squeezing under the snow layer and nibbling any leaves that they find.

On the Alps, the Andes, the Himalayas and the mountains of the Antarctic, there are some microscopic, pink, plant-like animals to be found living in moist snow. These are *Chlamydomonas nivalis*, snow algae. They exist in such large numbers in some places that the otherwise pristine white snow becomes an unbelievable shade of pink. Snow algae are called plant animals because they are able to fix the energy of the sun and turn it into sugar – like a plant – and also to swim in the water between the melting ice crystals, beating their whip-like tails, called flagella, like an animal. Each tiny alga has one eye, a red spot of pigment through which it is able to discern light and dark. It is therefore able to orientate itself into a position where there is sufficient light for it to photosynthesize. The pink pigment which floods the tiny body of the animal probably protects the underlying green chlorophyll, the key to the process of photosynthesis, from being destroyed by the effects of too much light. Snow algae have a very short life; growing, living, moving, mating and reproducing all have to be experienced before the onset of winter. The next generation spends the winter months warmly wrapped in a thick coat, in the form of resting spores, able to withstand the hardest winter.

When I was a girl, I lived in a house where there was no central heating. It was very cold on winter mornings and getting out of bed was a great effort, but the thing that made me jump out of my warm blankets eagerly was the prospect of seeing the beautiful frost patterns that had formed on the windows during the night.

Frost is composed of ice crystals formed when atmospheric water vapour condenses on a surface whose temperature is below 0°C (32°F). When frost forms, water vapour is changed directly to a solid, so the dew that clings to grass and trees, or the condensation on cold window panes, appears as a light deposit of ice, often in a delicate, feathery pattern.

Frost pockets occur in a valley bottom or smaller hollow. Dense, cold air is heavier than warm air, so it sinks and rolls to the bottom of a slope, where it accumulates. Such hollows in the landscape may have a much lower night-time temperature that the surrounding area, and often experience frosts earlier and later in the season.

WINTER BLUES

Primitive people lived close to nature, watching the skies and smelling the air, acutely aware of, and sensitive to, local atmospheric conditions. Their keen instincts and observations were passed on from generation to generation, but gradually our instinct for predicting the changes to come has diminished, and now we rely on meteorologists on radio or television to tell us what to expect in the way of weather.

The science that examines the influence of weather on living things is called biometeorology. Weather affects our comfort, well-being and mental state, particularly if we are old, very young or ill. But whatever our age or state of health, there are days when our spirits are high and all is well with the world; then on other days we feel so depressed that the best thing to do seems to be to stay in bed and be miserable in comfort! Researchers using an instrument called an algimeter have found that people feel pain more readily during changeable weather than they do in settled spells. Perhaps this is why some people predict a change in the weather when they feel rheumatic twinges, or when their bunions and corns are particularly tender.

For whatever reason, we are very sensitive to changes in the weather, though with many people the physical effect is slight.

In northern latitudes the lack of sunshine during December, January and February causes some people to suffer from a form of winter depression known as seasonally affective disorder (SAD). It is believed that the lack of sunlight increases the production of a hormone called melatonin and that this additional hormone causes clinical depression. The remedy is for the patient to sit in a room lit by a full spectrum light (2,000 lux), reading, working or relaxing, for some time each day. Not everyone is affected to this extent – an occasional sunny winter's day is usually enough to produce a feeling of well-being in most of us.

Many zoo animals, transported from tropical regions, have similar winter problems; besides

Norway spruce

being miserable throughout the period of short days they also become inactive and their circulation slows down. Our relatives, the primates, are likely to lose weight in winter; they are often listless and unco-ordinated and may suffer from diarrhoea, while we humans become more vulnerable to germs, catching colds and developing chest complaints.

Weather itself does not cause illness or disease, but it may be a contributory factor. The most important aspect of weather which affects the body is lack of heat. On cold days the body reacts by closing up the surface blood vessels, so that less blood reaches the body surface to cause loss of heat. This constriction causes the blood pressure to rise, and this may increase the clotting factor in the blood of those vulnerable to circulation problems.

The other real danger in cold weather is the wind chill factor, because strong winds have great cooling powers. The harder the wind blows, the greater the heat loss – you will discover this when, on very cold winter days, you try to keep the birds in your garden supplied with water. The bowl of water you put in an exposed, windy place will freeze faster than the water left in a sheltered position. It is tempting to wrap up with many layers of clothes against this sort of cold. But remember that it is important for the skin to be able to breathe, or the body will sweat; and the evaporation of the moisture cools the body at a fast rate. An animal's winter coat is of very thick fur, so that warm air is trapped around its body to make it feel warm, but not too hot. Air trapped in this way can be seen when an otter, water vole or water shrew swims, as the air gives the animal's body a silvery appearance.

PLUNGE INTO THE COLD

We know what is meant by winter; but when does it begin and when does it end? It is a season that creeps up on us when we are not looking and seems reluctant to slip away again in spring. As we have seen, it is the season of short days and long nights; a time when only a handful of flowers bloom and insects are few and far between. Many birds migrate to escape winter's chill, but others fly in from further north to escape even worse hardships; birds and mammals are easier to watch in winter, when hunger makes them bold and there is little cover. But all find the season a testing time and wherever we look in the countryside we see the struggle for survival.

WINTER OPTIONS

A nip in the early morning air foretells the threat of winter cold, while swallows, the heralds of summer, gather together to fly southwards to warmer lands. The tranquillity of autumn is shattered by rain and chill winds as a bleakness steals over the countryside.

A CHANGE IN THE LANDSCAPE

The habitat where an animal has lived throughout the summer gradually changes during autumn, often becoming an inhospitable place. Trees and shrubs lose their leaves, reducing the shelter provided by the woodlands, scrub and hedgerow. The loss of leaves means a loss of food for the insects that feed on them; and this in turn affects the invertebrates and birds that feed on the leaf-eaters. The invertebrates which normally live in trees and shrubs are deprived not only of food but also of their homes, so they must try to find hiding places amongst bare twigs and crevices in the bark. Another alternative is to drop to the ground and seek a refuge in the dead vegetation.

Invertebrates living in grassland and herbage throughout the spring and summer have a smaller choice of winter refuge than those living in trees. They could perhaps bury themselves in the ground, but most of them would come up against a problem. The heavy rains that we normally experience in autumn create a higher water table than that found in summer so, although the temperature of the soil in winter is higher than that above soil level, the prospects are not good unless the animal is adapted to very damp conditions.

Soil-dwelling animals, adapted as they are to variable soil conditions, are better at contending with wet winter surroundings, and they dig a little deeper below ground level. Worms, for example, were originally aquatic animals that invaded dry land; they die quickly if they are deprived of water. The die-back of ground vegetation leaves larger areas of bare soil for starlings, rooks, crows and blackbirds to patrol and forage for soil invertebrates, but their pickings will be meagre.

Animals which graze and browse, as well as those which feed on fruits and seeds, have to eat well on whatever remains at the beginning of winter, for new growth will not appear again before the end of February or the beginning of March. Rabbits, squirrels and

deer strip the bark from trees in order to reach the sappy layer underneath. As we have seen, this layer is part of the tree's food transportation system, so animals hungry enough to strip a tree's bark are rewarded with a rich feast of carbohydrates. This is fine for them, but not at all good for the tree.

Predators do not fare well in winter either; the herbivores they normally find in abundance, and capture with ease, are not very active; also the predators have little cover for stalking their prey and the potential victims are on their guard, as they, too, are exposed. The animals that do best in winter are those that eat carrion, as the death rate of birds and mammals is high. This increases the food supply of birds such as magpies and crows; foxes take carrion, too, as do any hungry badgers and moles.

Plants and animals have to be prepared for the cold and hunger that winter brings, and certain plants are so constituted that none of them survive even the mildest of winters.

PLANT LIFE IN WINTER

Not all flowering plants are adapted to overwintering; length of life generally depends on the species.

Annuals are plants that naturally live for less than a year. They grow, flower, set seed and die within a year, relying totally on seeds to ensure the continuation of their kind the following season. Field poppies, corn marigolds and corncockles are annual wild flowers, while cornflowers, sunflowers and sweet peas are among the many annuals to be found in a garden.

Ephemeral plants live for an even shorter time than annuals – sometimes as little as six to eight weeks from germinating from the seed to setting seed themselves, then dying. Many weeds are ephemeral, making them very difficult to eradicate from a garden, as they set seeds which germinate rapidly. Chickweed, shepherd's purse and groundsel are ephemeral plants.

Biennials devote their first year of life to growing and to storing nutritive materials; in their second year they flower and die. Foxgloves, teasels and mullein are biennials found in the wild, while hollyhocks, wallflowers and honesty are cultivated examples.

Perennial plants appear to be immortal; they flower each year after reaching maturity and because of their overwintering adaptations they are able to live for many years.

We have already looked at the way in which deciduous trees and

A fall of snow covers the earth like a blanket. Above, sounds are muffled and few animals are to be seen; but below the ground many creatures are active.

shrubs behave in winter, losing their leaves in order to conserve water. These plants have stout woody stems – the trunks – and branches; woody plants like these are always perennial. The stems of perennial herbaceous plants, however, are temporary structures which serve for one season only, then die back to grow again the following year. Examples of plants which behave in this way are cow parsley, hedge woundwort and marjoram in the wild, delphiniums, lupins and phlox in the garden. If these plants are to live through the winter they must have adaptations to help them survive. The roots, stems or leaves of herbaceous plants are cleverly modified to form overwintering structures which usually remain protected underground. The roots anchor the plant firmly in the soil and prevent it being blown over by the wind. They also absorb water and valuable mineral salts from the soil, and they can act as food stores.

Biennial plants, which only have to withstand one winter, form a single, central tuber; this stores the food, manufactured by photosynthesis during the first season, to keep the plant healthy throughout the winter and to fuel the reproductive activities of the following year. Carrots and parsnips are taproots full of stored food; in the wild similar roots can be found on thistles and all umbelliferous plants, including cow parsley, hogweed and rough chervil.

The commonest type of plant structure for overwintering is the rhizome. This is a creeping horizontal stem which usually grows underground and stores the plant's food supplies. Flag irises have rhizomes that lie along the soil surface; look carefully at the swollen stem of a flag iris and you will see leaf buds and leaf scars along its length. The short roots found on modified stems of this kind are called adventitious roots. Some rhizomes are long and slender, as in couch grass and herb paris; others are swollen like the flag iris's. Potatoes are tuberous swellings at the end of a thin rhizome; the eyes of the potato are lateral buds.

Crocus corms are short, stout, rounded bodies enclosed in papery brown scale leaves. When you plant crocus corms in the autumn, why not cut one in half to see how it works? You will see the swollen stem which contains stored food; it is sitting on top of last year's withered corm. Lateral buds grow from the sides of the corm; these are capable of growing into new plants, while the terminal bud on the top contains the leaves and the flower which will use the stored food to enable them to grow in spring.

A bulb is formed from a condensed shoot of stem and leaves. In this case it is the leaves which are modified for overwintering. The dry, brown outer leaves – the remains of last year's leaf-bases – protect the thicker inner ones, which are fleshy and succulent with stored food. In the heart of the bulb, protected by the white overlapping leaves, is the flower bud surrounded by the strap-like leaves that will grow up, with the flower, in spring. Snowdrops, daffodils and tulips have bulbs, but the one you will see most often and throughout the year is the onion bulb. Next time you cut one to put into a stew, look at the way it is structured – if you can see through your tears!

While many herbaceous plants 'vanish' from the garden and the countryside in winter, withdrawing the stock of nutrients from the leaves and storing them in overwintering organs, other perennial plants remain evergreen. This is because, on poor soils or in a harsh environment, leaves may not be able to manufacture much food for the plant in one season. It would be a drain on the plant's resources for it to lose all its leaves and have to begin growing new ones in spring. So the leaves must be tough enough to withstand the winter's frosts – they have to be strong, leathery or needle-like.

The seeds of many plants lie dormant throughout the winter, their hard seed cases protecting them from adverse weather conditions. Some of these seeds need a period of cold weather to stimulate them into growth in the spring, others need the frost to scarify them before the root and shoot can penetrate the casing.

Plants, the base of the food pyramid, must live to grow again or none of us would survive.

OPTING OUT

Migration is the movement of animals, seeds or spores from one area to another. But the movement of these individuals can be further divided into the categories of emigration – leaving a native habitat permanently; immigration – arriving in a new habitat; and migration – in the stricter sense of a periodic two-way movement to and from an area, often by well-defined routes.

When the Ice Ages began nearly 2,000,000 years ago, ice sheets and glaciers spread to cover most of Europe, North America and Asia as far south as the Himalayas. During the warmer interglacial periods, the ice melted and, when it did, the sea level rose; the landmasses of Europe and North America also rose, having been pressed down by the ice. The great weight and movement of the retreating glaciers carved out features in the landscape which are still visible today.

Throughout the time of the terrible cold, life continued above the ice sheets and around their margins. When the ice sheets eventually retreated, the hardy plants and animals which had survived close to the ice were the pioneers in the recolonization of the land underneath it. Those that were not so hardy had died of cold or been driven southwards, never to return. Many trees became extinct in Europe during the first Ice Age; interglacial deciduous forests were replaced in the succeeding cold phases by dwarf birches, Arctic willows and pine trees, with grasses and sedges scattered over the cold ground. Heat-loving animals such as elephants, hippopotamuses, rhinoceroses and bison emigrated, while woolly mammoths, cave bears and lemmings extended their territory southwards.

Even today, lemmings are famous for their spectacular emigrations. The Norwegian lemmings are the greatest travellers. Every three or four years they have a population explosion; Norwegian lemmings can produce several litters of young in a year, with between three and nine young in each litter. If the spring and autumn are mild and there is plenty of food – moss, grass, lichen, fruits and seeds – the majority of young survive. Breeding may continue into the winter if the weather is not too severe, and as there are few predators about in the cold weather, a huge population builds up by the following spring. The lemmings' burrows become overcrowded, with about twenty-five young in each family, and food begins to run out as the feeding grounds become too small to support the burgeoning populations. The lemmings don't wait around to die of starvation; instead, there is a mass exodus from the area. Under cover of darkness, a vast number of lemmings begin to move out in a furry stream, apparently with no particular destination in view. If the horde of animals encounters water, their normal reluctance to enter it is weaker than the force that drives them forwards. Lemmings can easily swim across a stream, but if they enter a wide river or a fjord they will drown. It would seem that this act of collective suicide is linked with restoring a natural balance in the population; certainly it is emigration, as there is no evidence to suggest that any surviving lemming returns to its home ground.

. . . OF BIRDS . . .

Maybe we are living through another interglacial age and our winters are practice periods for when the great cold strikes again! If this is so, then many birds are well versed in the art of avoiding winter weather; they migrate to warmer climes when the days grow short and the temperature begins to drop. The phenomenon of birds disappearing in the winter baffled ornithologists for a long time: it seems remarkable that as recently as 200 years ago, it was still thought that swallows and martins over-wintered in the mud at the bottom of ponds. The reproductive process of barnacle geese also remained a mystery for hundreds of years; it wasn't then known

that their breeding grounds were far away to the north, in Russia, Spitsbergen and Greenland. In a study of birds produced in 1639 there was an elaborate schematic drawing of the development of the barnacle goose, which, it would have us believe, developed from the stalked barnacles that cling to driftwood in the sea. It was thought that the little geese clung to the wood as barnacles and then, when they were large enough, they flew free as geese.

Birds that migrate do so in search of a continual supply of food in what would otherwise be a lean period. The summer multitudes of insects begin to disappear in autumn, when temperatures start to fall, and most of our insect-eating birds, such as swallows, martins and swifts, wouldn't stand a chance of finding enough food to keep them alive throughout the winter, so they move south to spend a few months in the tropics.

All European swallows cross the Sahara desert to overwinter in central and southern Africa, feeding as they journey southwards. Swallows from Germany and other parts of Central Europe winter mainly in central Africa, while those from Britain in the west and from Russia in the east journey on into the south of Africa. The swallows and sand martins of North America fly southwards to South America, and the barn swallow reaches Argentina and Chile. The cliff swallow, which breeds as far north as Alaska, overwinters in Brazil and Paraguay.

During October, a few years ago, we journeyed through America and into Mexico, where we travelled on the Copper Canyon railway from Chihuahua to Los Mochis near the west coast. After watching the sun set one evening, we mingled with the townspeople who were enjoying a festive occasion. I happened to look up and I couldn't believe my eyes, because every telephone wire was full of swallows, all sitting shoulder to shoulder. I found somewhere to sit and watch the birds; each one seemed to have a regular place where it perched. When another swallow came along it would fly directly to its perch and the others shuffled along to let the latecomer in. Occasionally a swallow would arrive which evidently did not have a regular perch in that area; when this happened the other swallows didn't make room and the incoming bird had to seek a place elsewhere.

I was so fascinated by the sheer numbers of swallows that I was up before sunrise to watch them again; this time the birds were leaving to forage for food in the surrounding countryside. Groups of swallows left together, taking off from the wires as though at a given signal. This reminded me of times when I have watched swallows gather on telephone wires before migrating; the question that always arises in my mind is where did swallows gather before the telephone was invented?

It seems incredible that a small bird like a swallow is capable of flying such long distances, but why ever do they come back again five or six months later?

The reason is that there are already many local birds in the tropics, and large numbers of birds arriving from the north would never be able to breed as well as compete for food alongside the natives. In Britain we have winter visitors, too, birds that fly in from their breeding grounds in Scandinavia, Iceland, Greenland and the inhospitable wastes of northern Russia and Asia, to spend the cold months in comparative comfort further south – in Ireland and on the west coasts of Britain, France, Spain and Portugal, where the land is lapped by the warm waters of the Gulf Stream. These northern birds are mainly geese, ducks and seabirds, but there are also some songbirds, including redwings, fieldfares and buntings.

The timing of the autumn migration is crucial; the adult birds of most species must have moulted and have their feathers in good condition after the busy breeding period, and the youngsters have to build up their strength in order to survive the journey. The urges to breed, to moult and to migrate are all triggered off by chemical changes that take place in the body; this same sort of biological timing mechanism induces the birds to feed more actively before beginning their travels.

Many migrating birds make their journey by daylight. Usually their routes south are influenced by the landscape: they funnel through mountain passes and cross short stretches of sea; coasts, rivers and valleys channel their passage overland. Sometimes the birds fly for a few hours, then spend a while feeding, but when they are flying before the advancing cold, they may not stop all day. The overland sections of their journey must be completed in stages of 150–300 km (90–190 miles) a day to keep ahead of the cold weather and to ensure that they reach their destination before their stored energy wanes. The birds fly about 200 metres (660 feet) above ground level and at this height they are clearly visible from below, so bird-watchers wait at various vantage points to see the wonderful sight of many birds passing overhead.

Birds which migrate by night are obviously not so easy to see, although on moonlit nights their silhouettes may be seen passing across the face of the moon. Radar operators are able to follow the course of the migration for long distances. It has been

curlews

54

registered that birds are unable to hold their course in strong winds, and that fog or thick cloud disorientates them. Radar has also revealed that the still air speed of most small migrant birds is no more than 35 km (22 miles) an hour. Larger birds are faster; blackbirds and starlings fly at 45–55 km (30–35 miles) an hour. According to the radar operators, night migration takes place beyond the range of human vision, often reaching heights of about 3000 metres (10,000 feet), although heavy rain makes it necessary for the birds to come down lower.

Nocturnal migrants may fly non-stop for three or four days, probably covering about 400 km (250 miles) in one stretch. Birds which do this, such as sedge warblers, store fat under their skin and use it to fuel their flight. Before starting out they may well have doubled their weight, so that at take-off in southern England they weigh 22 g ($^3/_4$ oz) and four days later, when they land in Senegal, south of the Sahara, they weight in at 10 g ($^1/_3$ oz).

Even when a bird has taken on plenty of food to fuel its journey, it has to be able to navigate correctly. Birds navigate by the sun and the stars, with help from the earth's magnetic field. Their long-used migration routes work well for them, and the birds have a built-in homing device and timing mechanism; they also have, within their genetic make-up, information crucial to accomplish their migration. This must be so, for, in the case of the cuckoo, the adults never meet their offspring – which have hatched in some other bird's nest – and they start out for Africa a month or two before the youngsters. The young birds fly alone on their first flight, so there must be *something* inside them telling them where to go. It is difficult to understand how a direction-finding mechanism such as this functions and, for all our technological advances, we still do not really know how these remarkable migrations are achieved.

The risks of spending a winter in northern latitudes are greater than those of a long migration journey; yet the dangers encountered are considerable. To be blown off course over land may not be too serious, but birds are likely to die if they are blown off course over the sea, or if the land they are making for is only a small island which they may never find. On dark nights migrating birds often fly into power cables that are carried on tall pylons. Aerial-bearing television towers supported by steel guys also take a horrific toll of birds; then there are lighthouses that dazzle them so that they fly into the building and are killed. Birds use traditional staging posts or resting areas, and this is all too often a disaster.

In the past, man killed migrating birds such as turtle doves, buntings, thrushes and warblers as necessary food. Today, in Cyprus, France, Spain, Portugal, Italy, Malta, the Lebanon, Syria and the Nile valley, there are hunters who spend a great deal of money on

monarch butterfly

their so-called sport, killing hundreds of thousands of birds each spring and autumn as they cross Mediterranean countries on their migration flights. This toll on the bird population, along with the destruction of their breeding sites, makes the future of migrating birds look grim.

...BUTTERFLIES AND MOTHS

It is difficult to imagine that the delicate fluttering of butterflies and moths could possibly enable the insects to migrate, but some species are stronger fliers than they appear and are quite capable of prolonged flight. Butterflies which are adapted to life in marshlands or on chalk hills rarely leave the area where they were born, as other similar habitats are few and far between; but those butterflies which put their eggs on widely occurring plants such as nettles and thistles tend to wander from habitat to habitat.

The seasonal movements of butterflies of temperate areas show a shift towards the poles in spring and summer, and towards the tropics in autumn. The stimulus seems to be a change in the length and temperature of the nights. Experiments have been carried out to prove that this is so: one involved the capture of large numbers of small white butterflies which were divided into two groups. The first was exposed to two successive long, cold nights; when the butterflies were released they began to migrate southwards. The second group was given two successive short, warm nights; on their release these butterflies flew north-north-west.

During the summer months, when there is plenty of food for caterpillars to feed on and the air temperature is warm, it takes only a few weeks for a butterfly's eggs to hatch, the caterpillars to grow and pupate and the next generation of butterflies to emerge. Small tortoiseshell, small white, large white and small copper butterflies are among those that produce more than one generation of adults a year. The embryo usually develops inside the egg within the space of a few days; the caterpillar stage takes from fifteen to thirty days, according to the species, and pupation at this time of year takes ten to fourteen days. So the transformation from egg to adult may take only four to six weeks.

The adult lifespan of most temperate butterflies is only about three or four weeks. So an individual butterfly, say a small white, emerges from pupation and, according to the length and temperature of the night, begins to fly across the countryside in a fairly constant direction. Each time it reaches a suitable habitat, such as a cabbage patch, it stays there for a short time. A male will leave immediately if there are no receptive females around; a female will probably lay a batch of eggs on the larval food plant before resuming her journey, providing the sun is still shining. This sequence continues throughout the individual's life. When the next generation of butterflies emerges from pupation, each of them too must decide which way to fly.

The major change in direction takes place in late summer and early autumn. The first butterflies to change course and begin to fly south are the large (cabbage) whites. They journey northwards in spring; the females lay eggs in May and June; then they die. The second generation of butterflies emerge from pupation in the middle of July or beginning of August, but instead of flying north-north-west, as their parents did, they fly in a south-south-easterly direction. Similarly second-generation red admiral and painted lady butterflies start their southward journey in mid-August. Butterflies living further south begin their migration slightly later: for example in north-eastern England a small white butterfly changes direction around 12 August; in southern England, the turn-around date is two weeks later, while in the Alsace region in north-eastern France the butterflies change direction at the beginning of September.

But how do migrating butterflies navigate? The answer is that they fly only during the warmest part of the day and when the sun is shining; detailed study has shown that they maintain a constant angle to the point on the horizon directly below the sun, known as the azimuth. Butterflies of temperate climates differ from birds, bees and tropical butterflies in that they do not compensate for the movement of the sun across the horizon. So although they gradually make their way across country in a more or less constant geographical direction, their flight path forms a series of gentle curves as they follow the sun. In this way a butterfly increases the area it flies over, making it more likely that it will find a habitat in which its larval plants may grow – in other words, a suitable place for a female to lay her eggs.

Butterflies are helped over stretches of water by air currents. On the east coast of Britain I have often seen hundreds of red admirals, and sometimes ladybirds, fly in from Europe, assisted by a following breeze. Like birds, however, butterflies can be swept off their chosen route by high winds; this can lead to some turning up in unexpected places and may account for the occasional appearance of rare species. From time to time a few monarch butterflies from North America arrive in the south of England, having been driven off course by high winds as they flew northwards towards the Great Lakes. This is an incredible journey for any butterfly to make, although monarchs are large by butterfly standards – their 110 mm (4$^1/_2$ in) wingspan makes them look like small, tawny birds when in flight.

The monarch is the most famous of the migrating butterflies,

The seasonal migrations of monarch butterflies involve journeys of several thousand kilometres.

because it makes a migration involving a similar return journey to those of migrating birds. At least part of that return journey is made by the same butterflies that travelled on the outward leg, as well as by their offspring – monarchs are comparatively long-lived, having an adult life of up to twelve months.

Throughout the summer the monarch is a common sight in the gardens and countryside of North America, but in late summer and early autumn it begins its journey south. This migration flight, from the Great Lakes in the north to Texas or the Gulf of Mexico in the south, covers between 2000 and 3000 km (1250–1850 miles). Many of the towns on the monarch's flight path have festivals or carnivals to celebrate the arrival of the butterflies. I have seen clouds of them flying southwards through Texas, with steady wing-beats. They were about 4–6 metres (15–20 feet) above the ground and travelled at about 17 km (11 miles) an hour. It was a never-to-be-forgotten sight.

The monarchs that reach Mexico spend the winter as free-flying, reproductive butterflies; they die within a few weeks of beginning to reproduce and it is their offspring that make the return flight north in the spring. The butterflies that do not fly far enough south to avoid being caught in a cold weather zone form spectacular, colourful 'butterfly trees', clustering together on evergreens so that the trees are completely festooned with roosting butterflies. In some forests in northern Mexico and southern California populations of hundreds of millions of monarch butterflies can be found clinging to trees and delighting the eyes of those who go to see them.

Then, from the beginning of March, most of the monarchs fly north, the females laying eggs as they go. During autumn and winter, they are not reproductively active, so they do not have to use up energy courting or laying eggs – they need only feed, rest and build up strength for their journey.

Some butterflies seen regularly in Britain cannot survive our winters, so their presence is due to migration from their main breeding areas around the Mediterranean. The painted lady has a wide distribution area and its life is marked by seasonal migrations. The European population emerges in the winter in the deserts of North Africa and starts the long journey through Europe, searching for thistles, mallows or nettles on which the females will lay their eggs. By July they may have spread as far north as Scandinavia. Having flown such a long way, some individuals may find themselves caught in a spell of very cold weather, so will hibernate where they are. But the majority have not flown quite so far and have time to return south, travelling up to 3000 km (1850 miles) to overwinter around the Mediterranean. The painted lady also makes long seasonal migration flights in North America, flying north in spring with the second generation returning to the warmer south in autumn.

Certain moths also migrate; these include the convolvulus moth and the hummingbird hawk moth, but as their flights take place at night they tend to escape notice. There are some moths, notably the silver-Y, which sometimes arrive from Africa in such numbers that their off-spring cause agricultural damage to crops of peas, lettuce and clover in central Europe. Although these moths reproduce successfully, they cannot survive the winter in northern climes.

. . . MAMMALS

Some terrestrial mammals migrate, too. Bison, wildebeest and spring-bok all move seasonally in search of food and water. The migration of deer is altitudinal – they move downhill to overwinter in sheltered valleys. In northern Europe reindeer also move to lower lying country where conditions are likely to be less severe, though some herds migrate towards the coast in autumn and return inland in spring. In the past, reindeer herds were followed by nomadic hunters who were dependent upon the animals for food and clothing, but that traditional lifestyle has largely been lost and today few people follow the ancient routes which have been in existence since the Ice Age. Other northern mammals, such as Arctic foxes and polar bears, are adapted for survival in one area throughout the year, as their fur provides protection from the cold; and a number of mammals are adapted to sleep through the harsh weather.

THE DEEP SLEEP OF HIBERNATION

When an animal finds itself in a cold environment it has to develop ways of keeping itself warm.

The key structure involved in the temperature regulation of warm-blooded animals is the skin. When an animal is exposed to the cold, heat will be lost from the body, but the body will respond in four ways to the potential heat loss. Firstly, fat stored under the skin acts as an insulator and reduces heat loss from the body. Animals which live in very cold habitats, such as polar bears and seals, have a very thick layer of this subcutaneous fat. Secondly, hair is raised and brought into a more or less vertical position, trapping air in the spaces between the hairs. This air is warmed by the body and forms an insulating layer around the animal. When a bird fluffs its feathers out on a cold winter's day, it is trapping air around its body.

Thirdly, in cold weather blood becomes diverted from the skin surface to the deeper layers when blood vessels in the skin constrict; this reduces loss of heat from the blood to the surrounding atmosphere. When this happens we go pale, or 'blue', with cold. Arctic explorers and mountaineers may be exposed to extreme cold for so long that skin cells die, resulting in frostbite due to prolonged absence of blood from the skin's surface. And finally, extra heat is produced by an increase in the metabolic rate which causes shivering and 'goose-flesh'. Vigorous exercise creates extra heat, too: even stamping our feet helps us to keep warm if we are standing around in the cold. In winter as much as 40 per cent of the energy provided by the food we eat may be used in generating heat when we are at rest.

The centre for controlling body temperature is a small area in the brain called the hypothalamus, which acts as a thermostat. But there comes a point when the body's ability to regulate its temperature breaks down. There is a critical temperature range which varies from species to species. If the temperature rises above the upper critical point, the animal dies of heat; below the lower critical point, it dies of cold. Animals which live in cold environments are therefore adapted to withstand lower temperatures than those animals living in a warm climate. If man had not developed the ability to make clothes he would not have been able to live in the temperate areas of the world – unless he had seasonally migrated or hibernated – because human beings have a low critical temperature level, not much below that of a desert rat!

As the low critical temperature is approached, the metabolic rate of the body increases. This means that more energy has to be used and more food is needed to fuel the energy. But if an animal can find a way of slowing its metabolic rate, it will not be under the same pressure to find food during winter when supplies are scarce. This is what happens during hibernation. The animal goes into a deep sleep. Its metabolic rate falls to the minimum needed to keep it alive; its body temperature drops; its heartbeat slows and breathing almost stops. It enters a state of suspended animation, becoming stiff and cold, almost as if it were dead. Temperature regulation does not stop completely, but the acceptable minimum is much lower than usual – rather like turning a thermostat down to a lower setting to save fuel.

All animals have to eat large amounts of food in late summer and early autumn in order to build up fat and so increase their chances of winter survival. Hibernators must have particularly large stores of fat in their body, to keep their systems ticking over during their long sleep. In some years, if the weather is bad in late summer and early autumn, hibernators cannot find enough food to increase their fat reserves to a safe level and they may die before the end of winter.

Hibernating mammals usually allow their body temperature to fall to that of their surroundings, so that their temperature fluctuates as the air temperature rises and falls. But if the air temperature falls to below freezing point, the hibernator's body functions switch on again, either to keep the body from freezing or to arouse the animal into activity to warm itself up. Arousal from hibernating sleep occurs quite often between November and March, and means that the animals need to eat in order to fuel the extra energy they are using. On mild winter nights hedgehogs snuffle around looking for food and you may even have seen bats hunting winter moths.

. . . HEDGEHOGS

As the days begin to shorten, hedgehogs search for hibernating sites amongst brambles, under a shed, in a shrubbery, in a compost heap or even in a pile of logs. They are quite likely to choose a potential bonfire, too, so beware of cooking a hedgehog when you want to burn your rubbish! A hedgehog may build several nests and then only use one of them. Maybe it can't make its mind up where the safest place will be; and of course if one nest were to be destroyed in some way, another would be useful. It gathers fallen leaves, grasses and bracken and makes a ball of the materials; the nest ball is then pushed against something firm such as tree roots or stems surrounding the nest site. The hedgehog burrows into the middle of the ball and turns round and round, making the nest compact, with a central sleeping chamber which is made to measure, well insulated and protects the occupant from freezing. Hedgehogs overwinter alone, rolled into a ball, with nose and legs tucked away into the warm fur of the underside.

Four years ago, when I was digging in my wild garden on a December day, I dug up a hibernating hedgehog. I was concerned about this, as disturbance can mean death to animals in this state. I put the hedgehog in a box of grass under the hedge while I thought about what to do. I had been making a wall, the sort of wall that leans back against a bank of soil; my idea was that this would be a good place for mice, voles and solitary bees and wasps to live, besides being a useful thing to do with the materials I was digging up from the ground. So, at the end of this wall I

hibernating hedgehog

added a hedgehog cave made of stone. It is about 38 cm (15 in) square, with a passageway leading to the garden 15 cm (6 in) high and the same wide. The roof is made of a large flat stone that I can lift up if I want to peep inside, and the narrowness of the passageway means the hedgehog is safe from most predators. I say 'most' because there is another wall in the garden which is home to a weasel, and I really don't trust him. However, I lined the hedgehog cave with dry grass and leaves and put the hedgehog into the protected space. I know it fared well because I kept looking to see, and in February it came out, ate a saucer of cat food, had a drink of water and, after ambling around for a while, returned to the nest. Since then there has been a hedgehog in the cave every winter.

. . . BATS

A male pipistrelle bat will weigh about 6.25 g (just under ¼ oz) at its fattest time, at the beginning of October, and will lose weight steadily until it weighs only 3.75 g (⅛ oz) in April. In other words it will lose over a third of its weight during the winter, by using up its fat reserves. Imagine my concern, then, when one evening at the end of August someone brought me an injured pipistrelle bat. This was the time it should have been hunting and feeding actively to put on lots of weight; instead it had become hooked on a fishing line by a boy who was practising casting. The hook had torn the bat's wing-membrane, but fortunately these heal quite quickly. Bats can and do bite, but if you hold a bat with its back in the palm of your hand and its head projecting between your two forefingers it seems to feel secure and doesn't wriggle.

I prepared a vivarium as a temporary home for it, with a piece of stiffened gauze fastened at one end for it to cling to. The first evening it was with us I fed it on blood-worms, as these were the only things I had available for it to eat. The next day we bought a carton of meal-worms; the bat took these from my fingers as greedily as a child with a bag of sweets. I had to teach it to eat from a dish, so that I could leave enough food for it to eat if it became hungry when I wasn't around. This wasn't a difficult task. Over a period of about three days, I gradually lowered my fingers a little each time I fed the bat, until they were among the meal-worms in the dish; the bat got the idea and from then on fed well without help. I gave it moths, flies and anything else I thought it would normally eat, alongside the meal-worms. It was strange seeing it flop around the floor of the vivarium; bats are so elegant in flight, but surprisingly clumsy on a flat surface.

By mid-October, the pipistrelle was fit enough to be put into an old shed in the garden. Gradually it became less dependent on my food offerings and I was very pleased when it disappeared in time to hibernate in the roof of the house with the rest of its kind.

For their hibernation roost, bats choose a cold place where conditions are stable. A draught-proof cave or a roof space is ideal. As the time for hibernation draws closer, the bats emerge from their roost less frequently to feed. Gradually they slip into a state in which the heart, pulse and breathing rate are so reduced that very little energy is needed to maintain them. Their body temperature then falls to match that of their surroundings, again reducing energy requirements. Bats are very vulnerable to disturbance in winter; if they are forced into activity, the fuel they burn during the waking period may reduce their reserves to a level that is inadequate for their survival.

. . . DORMICE

When we lived in East Sussex we were fortunate in having common dormice in the garden. Although they are called 'common' dormice, they are not at all common in England and we were pleased to have them around.

Dormice make summer nests of grass and strips of honeysuckle bark, but the winter nest, built in October for their solitary hibernation, is made of moss, leaves and grass woven together and hidden in the shelter of roots or in piles of fallen leaves. We had to be careful in the garden, as the dormice enjoyed overwintering in the warmth of the compost heap or in the manure pile, and they were in danger of my digging them into the soil.

Dormice feed hugely in autumn, in order to fatten themselves up and build up reserves for the winter. The common dormouse eats nuts – particularly hazelnuts – flowers, fruits and a few insects; garden dormice eat autumnal fruits and nuts, together with insects and snails (in summer they also take any eggs or small nestlings they find). The fat dormouse lives up to its name and becomes very plump on fruits, seeds and nuts.

As October progresses, dormice sleep for a longer and longer time each day, until the time comes when it is too cold for them to go out and hunt for food. We have found them curled up as though dead, chin on fat stomach, legs tucked in, furry tail curled over the head like a scarf. Dormice avoid the hard season by means of a deep, coma-like sleep, which may last for up to six months. They may wake up if the temperature is especially mild for some time in the winter, but this does not often happen. The rate of their bodily functions drops and

A mallard ripples into the icy water of a sheltered pond. Ducks choose their mates in October and the pair stays close together within the flock.

their body temperature falls to little above freezing, but, if you listen very hard, you can hear a tiny whistling snore! This snoring may lead to death, as badgers, foxes and even magpies are sometimes able to locate dormice, whereupon they dig them up and eat them.

. . . SNOOZES

Bears which live in cold regions spend the winter in a deep sleep, known as winter dormancy. This is not true hibernation, as the heart rate does not slow down very much and the body temperature lowers by only a few degrees. The sleep is a method of coping with a time when food is short; and an active bear needs much more food than a bear that sleeps and survives on fat built up during autumn.

The brown bear is the largest land carnivore and, because it had no serious rival until the coming of man, it used to be widespread across Europe, Asia and North America. In Europe it is still to be found in large numbers in Scandinavia and Russia; but elsewhere in Europe it has been reduced to small, isolated populations in eastern Poland, Slovakia, the mountains of Italy, the Pyrenees and the Picos de Europa mountains of north-western Spain. In most of these countries bears are either totally protected or can only be shot under licence. In North America brown bears and black bears live in the wilder, un-inhabited areas and in national parks. These two bear species both have periods of winter dormancy and, as their habits are not dis-similar, I shall concentrate on the brown bear, which is to be found in both continents.

Male and female brown bears look alike, though the female is slightly smaller than the male. They are uncommonly strong animals and the muscles of the neck, back and forefeet are particularly powerful, but for such a large, heavy animal the brown bear is remarkably agile, too. It is able to break into a run when it is attacking prey or escaping from man, but its usual speed is a steady amble; it also has an odd way of sitting on its rump and shuffling about when gathering fruit and berries or feeding on other ground vegetation. The fact that the bear is capable of standing upright on its hind feet and shambling forwards in an almost human gait may well account for its fascination for many people; but this posture is usually adopted only when it is necessary to spy out the land.

Brown bears do not defend their territory with as much zeal and ferocity as most other territorial species, and two bears may share the same hunting grounds. The animal's diet varies from season to season; in spring the bears of the forest eat tubers, roots and rhizomes, truffles and other fungi. The brown bear is an opportunist hunter of meat whenever it is available; birds, mammals, fish, worms, amphibians and

crossbill

insects are all part of its diet. However, in autumn bears eat fruit and nuts with great relish, and honey is a special treat. These large amounts of food must be washed down with plenty of water; brown bears cannot tolerate excessive drought or heat.

For most of the year the brown bear uses a number of lairs, not making them at all comfortable and often moving home. But as winter approaches it carefully selects one refuge, which may be a south-facing cave or an area of dense undergrowth deep in a forest. Should the entrance to the cave be too wide, the bear heaps up branches and moss to leave only a small aperture. Inside the den, it looks for the driest place and scoops out a depression which it fills with grass and dead leaves, making a warm, snug nest in which to sleep through the cold weather.

It is difficult to predict when a bear will retire for the winter, as this depends on the locality and the climatic conditions in any particular year. December is often the beginning of the rest period, and at this time the bear leaves its den from time to time to defecate and urinate; as it eats less, excretory activity diminishes, but the brown bear is an animal of clean habits and still has to go out of doors to urinate. For the rest of the winter it becomes lethargic, sleeping for much of the time, but waking on fine, sunny days and occasionally being tempted to venture outside.

A STATE OF TORPOR

We saw earlier that reptiles and amphibians – 'cold-blooded' creatures – became more or less animated according to the temperature they found themselves in. In the tropics, these animals remain active all the year round; but in Britain and northern Europe, where winter brings little warmth and food is in short supply, the animals become sluggish. While comparatively few northern European mammals adopt the extreme course of hibernating to ensure winter survival, all our reptiles and amphibians spend the winter months in a deep torpor, to avoid freezing to death.

During mid-autumn, when the nights begin to grow cold, reptiles find winter quarters in disused burrows, dry holes in a bank, hollows under stones or logs, crevices among tree roots, the warmth of a pile of leaves or a compost heap. Once settled into such a retreat, the reptile's body temperature, heart rate and breathing drop until the animal is only just alive and it drifts into a torpor. In this state it looks and feels dead. Unusually severe winter conditions kill many reptiles, but strong individuals which are well insulated from the frost survive.

Amphibians, that is frogs, toads and newts, overwinter in or out of water. Many frogs and some newts bury themselves in the mud at the bottom of a pond or ditch. Although these animals have lungs, and when on land they breathe in air through nostrils, when they are over-wintering under water they absorb enough oxygen through their skin to enable them to remain submerged, at a time when their bodily functions are almost at zero. Toads, and some frogs and newts, look for a winter retreat on land – in an old mouse or vole hole, a cellar or a garden shed, cracks and crevices covered by leaves, or a compost heap. Wherever they choose to overwinter, they fall into a state of torpor. Unlike mammals, which lose weight during hibernation, amphibians and reptiles wake up in early spring having lost very little weight and ready to begin the breeding season.

Hummingbirds are very active little creatures. They take in nectar and eat many insects during a typically busy day, but at nightfall they lower their body temperature and fall into a torpor in order to save energy. When the birds are sitting on their roosts in a torpid state, they do not respond to any sound or movement, however close. It is only the rise in temperature that comes with the light of dawn that will restore them to their normal flurry of activity. The word 'noctivation' has been used to describe this overnight torpidity, and it is similar to the longer period of inactivity, hibernation.

I have been fortunate in being able to see hummingbirds in Africa, North America and Mexico, but I think the ones I found most fascinating were those that were journeying over 3200 km (2000 miles) to overwinter in Central America. The rufous hummingbird measures only 10 cm (3.75 in) and weighs a meagre 4 g ($^1/_7$ oz); it breeds as far north as southern Alaska, but when the days grow shorter and food supplies dwindle it begins to fly south. It flies along the west coasts of Canada and the United States, through Mexico – where I saw it – and down into Central America, where it recuperates for a few months. Many of these birds may live for ten years and they repeat this migration flight twice a year for the whole of their lives. The calliope and the ruby-throated hummingbird, both tiny birds, also make long, twice-yearly journeys from North to Central America. Some human beings won't even walk to post a letter – they have to go by car!

TIME FOR THE ANTI-FREEZE

We have seen how the painted lady, the monarch and some other species of butterfly fly southwards to avoid unfavourable weather conditions. But what happens to other insects when there is no food available, the days are short and the temperature is low?

Some insects go into a sort of dormancy, similar to that seen in plants; it is known as diapause. It happens when the insect's body stops producing the hormone which promotes development. The hormone production is related to day length: as soon as the hours of daylight fall below a certain level, diapause begins, though the critical amount of daily light needed to trigger it varies from insect to insect.

Diapause can take place at any stage of an insect's life – egg, larva, pupa or adult – to protect the creature during an unfavourable period. For example, the summer caterpillars of the cabbage white butterfly pupate for about two weeks before the adult butterflies emerge. But when the autumn caterpillars go into pupation, they begin a diapause which lasts from October till the following May – that is about eight months before the adults emerge. The vapourer moth overwinters in the egg, the yellow underwing as a caterpillar, the dagger moth as a pupa, and the brimstone butterfly as an adult.

Insects are 'cold-blooded' and so their temperature is determined by the external environment. Each species of insect has a minimal temperature threshold below which it cannot survive; so when the insect begins to prepare for winter survival, it produces a substance called glycerol which is added to the haemolymph, the insect equivalent of blood. Glycerol acts like anti-freeze, lowering the insect's freezing point and also protecting the body tissues from being damaged by the cold. If you have ever found a caterpillar or a butterfly during the winter, or if you have dug a moth pupa up from the soil, you will know that it feels icy cold and is quite brittle; this is the anti-freeze doing its work. We usually have a few lace-wings sitting the winter out on our ceilings; they turn pink during their diapause, and when spring comes they return to their normal green colour.

Not all insects sleep through the winter. On mild days winter moths and winter gnats are to be seen, while other invertebrates hide under plant pots and logs in the garden. The stems of umbellifers and reeds, and large tufts of grass, are good overwintering places for insects which venture out on the milder days; but many more insects die, leaving their eggs to survive the winter and begin a new generation.

Waterlife in Winter

Motionless water with banks of withered reed beds and bare bending trees, drab and dull, grey and brown. A sudden rattle of wings, a flurry of hoar crystals and a mallard ripples into the icy water, bringing a bright sheen of feathers and a poetry of movement to the winter pond.

CHANGING THE FACE OF THE HABITAT

Freshwater habitats seem so still and silent in winter. The floating leaves of water lilies and pondweed have disappeared; instead, fallen leaves and broken twigs are scattered over the cold grey ripples. Whirligig beetles, those miniature powerboats of the water surface, are buried in the mud safe from the harsh weather, and the water striders are hibernating amongst the withered vegetation.

Winter, when we expect a good deal of rain and perhaps some snow, brings a change to some terrestrial habitats. During heavy rain, water flows into the tiny gaps between the soil particles and fills them completely, so that the soil becomes saturated: for the time being it will absorb no more water. If the land is well drained, this water will seep down through the soil, leaving each soil particle with a film of water around it and the gaps between the particles full of air once more, ready to cope with the next downpour. The water that drains away is called gravitational water. It flows into the earth as far as it can and then collects to form an underground reservoir called the water table; this is the natural level of water that is underground at any given place.

Damp hollows and dune slacks hold water throughout the winter, encouraging ducks and wildfowl to explore their possibilities. The level of permanent water in ponds, lakes and rivers rises with the winter rains, flooding water meadows and low-lying land. Earthworms rise in the soil beneath the flood water and become food for visiting snipe; dabbling ducks such as mallards and gadwall enjoy these shallow-water conditions too. As the volume of water in rivers and streams increases, so does the speed of the moving water, causing problems for some animals living in the turbulence, such as otters, water shrews and water voles, and uprooting some marginal plants.

The kingfisher dives into pools to catch its prey, but it must go hungry when its fishing ground is covered in ice.

WATER PLANTS IN WINTER

Plants such as water crowfoot, water violet and water-lily have their roots anchored into the bottom of their habitat; they are able to produce leaves at any level in the water, from the base of the plant to the water surface. The underwater leaves of these plants are protected from the winter weather by the surrounding water; but free-floating plants such as frogbit or duckweed must have a specialized overwintering system in order to survive.

Frogbit has spreading, heart-shaped leaves that rest on the water surface in the form of a small rosette. These leaves provide a habitat for many small animals on which fish feed, and they usually carry snail spawn. The plants spread as strawberries do, putting out shoots known as stolons whose terminal bud produces a new rosette of leaves and roots and further stolons, until one plant has become a floating raft of many plants. In autumn, the most recently formed stolons terminate in solid, heavy, egg-shaped winter buds which hang down in the water. These winter buds, or turions, contain embryonic frogbit plants and a store of starch; they are the future generation. The turions break away from the parent plant and fall through the water to lie dormant in the mud until the water temperature rises in spring; then the reserve of starch enables the winter buds to spread their tiny leaves. The many air spaces in the leaf tissues make the little plants buoyant, so they can rise to the surface and continue their growth there.

Duckweeds are very small plants composed of a leaf-like 'body' called a thallus and a tiny thread-like root. In autumn starch is stored in dark, thickened thalli and these, like the turions of frogbit, fall to the bottom of the habitat to overwinter. Other water plants, such as reedmace and flag iris, store food in their roots and remain dormant until spring, when the food is used to produce shoots and growth is resumed.

As water plants die back during the autumn, their leaves and stems gradually fall around the water margins and into the habitat, forming thick layers, rich in organic matter. Because of this, litter feeders such as springtails, some mayfly nymphs, stone flies and water slaters, have plenty of food. Other invertebrates gather among the underwater litter layers, too; dragonfly nymphs and some water beetles and water bugs hunt their herbivorous prey in this area of plentiful food. In the cold conditions of winter their life processes slow down, so they require less oxygen and move more slowly.

A TOUCH OF ICE

In winter, the temperature of water is not as cold as that of the air above it; nor is it as warm in summer. Under the water surface the temperature falls very slowly, because water is a poor conductor of either heat or cold; so water animals do not suffer the sudden changes in temperature that land animals sometimes have to endure. When a layer of ice forms over the water surface, the water below is even more insulated from the cold atmosphere above, unless severe conditions continue for some time. A thin ice layer does not impede the passage of light, so the submerged plants can still photosynthesize.

A by-product of photosynthesis is oxygen; and this may be a critical factor in keeping the habitat aerated when atmospheric oxygen is unable to diffuse into the water. Should the ice layer thicken to more than 5 cm (2 in), or if snow falls and settles on the ice, there is too little light for the plants to photosynthesize and carbon dioxide is produced instead of oxygen. However, because cold slows down the activities of cold-blooded animals, fish are able to survive for a few days with little oxygen, staying close to the mud at the bottom of a pond when the water above them is almost all frozen solid. But fish die in large numbers from oxygen deficiency when snow and ice cover their habitat for long periods, nor can animals survive if they become frozen into the ice layer. Fish, freshwater mussels and snails are among the animals which seek to overwinter in deep water that will not freeze solid; while water insects which hibernate safely in the mud have 'anti-freeze' in their blood like their terrestrial counterparts.

Breaking the ice on a pond is very damaging to the animals living underneath. The impact of the breaking ice sends shock waves through the water and these hit the animals hard; fish and hibernating frogs can be killed or concussed in this way. If you want to make a hole in the ice in a frozen pond, pour hot water on to a small area.

A RIVER WALK IN WINTER

Most birds are able to survive short periods of harsh weather by utilizing the fat deposits laid down under the skin in autumn, but few can withstand severe winter conditions for long. Waterside birds probably suffer most when their food supplies are sealed below a layer of ice.

I count myself lucky when I see the resident kingfisher on my walks by the river. Kingfishers live along streams with high banks, canals, ponds, lakes and flooded gravel pits, wherever there is a good supply of sticklebacks and minnows. A kingfisher often sits motionless on a perch in a strategic position overlooking the water; or sometimes it may hover over a pool, watching for the movement of a small fish, a water beetle or an aquatic insect larva. Suddenly there is a flash of iridescent blue-green and the small rainbow-coloured bird drops into the water, reappearing in seconds with its prey in its beak. It beats sticklebacks against its perch until they are dead and the dorsal spines lie flat along the back. Fish are always eaten head first, as eating a fish tail first would force the gills and scales back and choke the kingfisher; so it juggles with its victims to ensure they go down the right way.

Male and female kingfishers occupy different territories out of the breeding season; the sexes look alike, but the male's bill is all black while the female has an orange-red lower mandible. During harsh winters many kingfishers die of cold and starvation; but a worse threat to this beautiful bird is from water pollution and the removal of river-bank trees, which afford perches, privacy and nesting possibilities among the root systems.

The dipper is a stocky, thrush-shaped bird of fast-flowing streams. All through the winter its clear voice can be heard, warbling a song of territorial possession. One of my favourite walks, at all times of the year, takes me along a river-bank where I can watch a dipper fishing. It stands on a boulder with water foaming all around, curtseying to the river before it plunges in, diving through the water using its short wings as fins. It is wonderful to stand on a bridge and see this dark bird walking into the current under the river, wings angled, searching for the invertebrates adapted to life in fast-flowing water. Up bobs the dipper, firmly gripping a stonefly nymph or a caddis larva, blinking the water from its eyes with a white membranous eyelid. Dippers and kingfishers both have soft, dense plumage for insulation; but when icicles hang from the bending trees and water plants are ringed with ice, how I shiver for these birds that have to dive into the cold winter waters in order to live!

Grey wagtails share the same stretch of river as the dipper; it is an area of boulders and deep pools just below a weir, where the river quietens and becomes more peaceful. Despite their sombre name, grey wagtails are bright birds in every way: they are nimble, with tails that twitch continually as they search for insects; they have elegant, streamlined bodies, grey-blue above and lemon yellow below. Males have a black throat-patch in the breeding season, but after the autumn moult the pairs look alike. In winter the birds become more gregarious and groups roost together for warmth. Some grey wagtails leave their usual haunts in late autumn and may be seen around sewage farms and cress beds, where more insects are to be found, but they are seldom far from a tumbling stream or a weir.

Moorhens and coots also live on this stretch of river, but they are to be seen in the peaceful, slow-moving water above the weir. The moorhens are secretive and skulk in the vegetation along the bank; they are reluctant to fly, and if they are disturbed they scuttle across the water surface anxiously calling, 'Kittik-kittik-kit-kit', a sound that always reminds me of breaking ice. When they swim they have an attractive way of jerking their heads backwards and forwards, emphasizing the red forehead and yellow bill; they flick their tails, too, showing the white flashes down the sides as they rapidly make their way back to the shelter of the overhanging trees.

By contrast, the coots are aggressive and in the breeding season they have a strong territorial sense; in winter, however, they are quieter and more gregarious. Coots are identifiable by their white foreheads and large, lobed feet, which make them clumsy on land. They, too, are reluctant to fly and prefer to run frantically over the water surface, the powerful feet scattering water before the bird crash-dives for safety. Moorhens and coots eat seeds, water weeds and all kinds of invertebrates, and are preyed on by foxes, which hunt the river-banks for the waterfowl. In severe winters large numbers of coots move to coastal waters, but in more normal conditions they stay put, taking the rough with the smooth in their own stretch of water.

Mallards inhabit all parts of the river. These ducks are found in ponds in towns, parks and villages, in gravel pits, reservoirs, lakes, estuaries and salt marshes. Just in case their numbers need swelling, immigrants arrive from western Europe to overwinter in Britain. In autumn the mallards begin to pair up. October is a good month to watch the displays, when the drakes, splendid in their breeding plumage, swim low in the water, flicking their heads, jabbing their bills into the water, splashing and showing off their black, curled tail feathers. When the ducks approach, the drakes often respond by rearing out of the water, stretching their necks and whistling. A duck will choose the drake which, in her eyes, is displaying most vigorously; she bobs her head to one side and swims close by him. The rejected males begin to squabble and lunge at each other with their bills; this often frightens the duck, which may fly off, followed by several amorous drakes. Mating takes place in November and once the pair are bonded they stay close together within the group or flock.

I think herons must have endless patience. I pass one most days on my walk; it stands motionless, 'shoulders' hunched, bayonet-shaped bill pointing towards the shallow water, a solitary grey sentinel waiting for a fish, perhaps an eel, to swim by. Many herons die in severe winters, when ice prevents them from catching

dipper

food; but many more die when their feeding ground becomes polluted by toxic chemicals, as when agricultural spray run-off seeps into the watery habitat. Sometimes I startle the heron; then it slowly and majestically takes to its broad, rounded wings, flapping away to soar and glide and come to rest further up the river.

I enjoy bird-watching at Leighton Moss in Lancashire. Last year we were lucky enough to see some bearded tits, or reedlings as they are sometimes called. These little birds hang on to the reeds, peering around; then suddenly they are away, fluttering in and out of the reed stems, calling to each other with a bell-like 'ping'. The male birds have grey-lilac heads and dark facial stripes, more like moustaches than beards, while the female has a brown head and no moustache. Bearded tits are restricted to life in wetlands where there are large reed beds. They have to change their diet in order to survive the winter; so, when insects disappear in autumn, bearded tits move from reedhead to reedhead, picking out the seeds and maybe finding the occasional hibernating insect. The bird's stomach has to expand in winter to accommodate the change in diet; but when snow and ice encapsulate the reedheads, making the seeds within unobtainable, bearded tits are unable to find alternative food and soon die of starvation.

I rarely walk along the riverside without seeing a water vole. Some people call these animals water 'rats', but they really are voles, with rounded, guinea pig-like features, small, neat ears and a short tail. In the stillness of a winter's morning you may hear a water vole crunching the root of a waterside plant, or you may see one sitting in a hunched position, holding the food it is eating in its forepaws. The main food of water voles is the stems and leaves of grasses and other plants that grow close to the river's edge; but sometimes there are the remains of freshwater mussels or water snails scattered around the usual feeding station. In autumn the animals often store roots and plant stems in their burrows, presumably to eat when fresh food is difficult to find or when snow and ice make foraging unrewarding. Water voles are expert swimmers and divers, but they only swim to escape from danger. All four feet are used in a sort of dog-paddle and only the top of the head, the back and the tail break through the water surface. Sometimes, if the water vole is very frightened, it dives to the bottom of the river and scrabbles the mud up, creating a form of smoke screen to enable it to swim rapidly to the underwater entrance of its home. The water vole has many predators, including brown rats, stoats, weasels, birds of prey, herons and pike.

Occasionally in winter I come across the body of a water shrew that has died of cold and starvation. Many young water shrews die during their first winter, often because of a lack of experience; but even those that survive rarely live more than two years. They do not grow a winter coat the second time around, and their teeth become worn down and useless. The coat of a water shrew is so water-repellent that the animal bobs like a cork on the water; when it dives, the air trapped in the fur covers the slate-black coat with a film of silver bubbles and the little animal has to paddle all the time it is searching for food amongst the stones and water weeds, or it would be carried back to the surface.

Water shrews have to work very hard to find enough food to maintain their body temperature; they must eat their own body weight every twenty-four hours. Earthworms, insects, small fish and plant materials are all part of a water shrew's diet; they even paralyse frogs with a lethal bite, which injects a venomous saliva – the frog is then eaten with ease. This constant activity puts a high demand on the heart and circulatory system, so it is hardly surprising that their life expectancy is so short. Foxes, owls and predacious fish, such as pike and perch, eat water shrews.

A BREATH OF SEA AIR

We visited Morecambe Bay in Lancashire on a cold day in late September. The hills of the Lake District were swathed in a mist of rain, while the nearer hills were folded in shades of grey against a pearl sky. Flocks of starlings were wheeling and ebbing, closing and spreading above us; two herons stood isolated on the salt marsh.

The tide was coming in and only a thin rim of sand remained. This was covered by a rippling carpet of birds; there were oystercatchers, plovers, knots, dunlins, curlews, lapwings, black-headed gulls, great black-backed gulls, golden plovers and redshanks. At the edge of this bird congregation, three sandpipers busily dipped their long bills into the wet sand, occasionally fluttering nervously away from the throng, but always staying together.

Hundreds of thousands of birds were standing in the shallow waters of the rising tide, all facing the wind so that their feathers did not get ruffled. Above the salt marsh the land rose, thorn-covered, the vegetation shaped by the wind. A heron came in to land, disturbing hundreds of birds as its huge wings spread raptor-like above them.

As the tide crept up to the marsh, birds began to fly, gathering others with them to drift like a plume of smoke further down the bay where some sand still

grey wagtails

remained uncovered. At high tide a dark shroud of birds spread over the cord grass and glasswort of the salt marsh, all of them still facing into the wind.

WADING BIRDS

Late August, September and October are the best months to see wading birds collecting on estuaries before a proportion of them fly south to spend the winter in warmer climes. The birds delay departure as long as possible, gaining weight and resting after a summer of nesting and raising their young.

Estuaries all over Europe give vital refuge to huge numbers of over-wintering wading birds and wildfowl, as well as providing year-round habitats for many other birds and fish. Estuaries are places where rivers meet the sea. In most estuaries the heavier, denser salt water floods along the bottom of the channels, while the lighter fresh water flows in a layer above the salt. But in some, notably the estuaries of such rivers as the Severn, the Seine and the Amazon, and in the Bay of Fundy in eastern Canada, after low tide, salt water moves forward in a great surge or bore (sometimes called an eagre), mixing completely with the fresh water. As the river flows towards the sea, it picks up loose rocks, boulders and silt and carries them along in the strength of its flood; but as it nears the coast it loses the energy to transport heavy weights and meets the sea carrying only mud and silt suspended in the water. When the fresh water and sea water meet, the suspended particles of sediment are attracted to each other by a process known as flocculation; as the accumulating groups of sediments become bigger and heavier they fall, and over a period of time the mud level is raised into banks. In the course of hundreds of years a natural succession takes place around an estuary, from bare flat mud to mudbanks which over many years become salt marsh; in its turn, over centuries the salt marsh endeavours to become firm land.

The tidal rhythm rules the lives of the plants and animals living in an estuary. The inhabitants of these areas of varying salinity must be highly specialized to cope with life in a habitat where twice in every twenty-four hours the salt tide washes in, and where after heavy rain there is a higher proportion of fresh water for a time. Soft mud is easy

Curlews call as they fly over a lonely beach, while other birds probe into the mud below the shallow water. The vast numbers of invertebrate animals which live in the mud or sand of the shore provide an important food supply for many fish and wading birds.

to burrow into and vast populations of crustaceans, marine worms and molluscs lie concealed in the mud, probing from the safety of their burrows to feed in the tidal waters. Sandhoppers, which are amphipod crustaceans – that means they have distinct pairs of feet for swimming and for jumping – lie in their U-shaped burrows, taking food from filtered water when the tide is out and scavenging on the muddy surface when the tide is in. Lugworms and ragworms are among the many estuarine worms which live in this habitat; the lug-worm feeds on detritus from the shelter of a burrow, while the rag-worm is an active predator, catching shrimps and other small creatures. Tiny snails of the genus *Hydrobia* feed on the mud surface when the tide is out, burrowing beneath the surface for safety. Peppery furrow shells, common cockles, Baltic tellins and many other burrowing bivalves filter food from the surface of the mud or sand, while mussels and oysters lie in their communal beds and sift food from the muddy waters. The multitudes of invertebrates living in the estuarine mud or in the sand are an important food supply for many fish and for birds, which eat both the invertebrates and the fish.

Wading birds feed mainly on crustaceans, worms and molluscs, and this is why there are so many of them around estuaries, especially in winter. All wading birds breed in the northern hemisphere and all are migratory; many of them cross the equator to overwinter. Britain and Ireland are sufficiently far north to provide breeding grounds for some waders, but also far enough south to be the overwintering grounds for others. Europe and America share many of the same species of shorebirds, either as breeding species or visitors.

Wading birds have a number of characteristics in common: all have long legs and long-toed feet in relation to their body size; many have long, slender wings, adapted to fast and long-range flight. In winter most wading birds have drab plumage colours, affording camouflage against their habitat background of mud-flats, sandy beaches or estuaries. There are, of course, exceptions to this general rule: the woodcock retains its russet-barred camouflage throughout the year, blending perfectly with the undergrowth of damp woodlands in which it lives its secretive life. Glossy lapwings, gleaming purple-green, and speckled golden plovers gather on farmland, where they search for insects and worms, though they are sometimes also seen on mud-flats and seashores during mild spells in winter.

When there are so many hundreds of thousands of birds to be seen, it is difficult to imagine how they can possibly find enough food to sustain them all throughout the winter. But there are innumerable invertebrates living in the mud, and in autumn their numbers are at a peak. It seems incredible, but surveys show that in a square metre (just over a square yard) of estuarine mud, the following densities may be found: up to 600 ragworms, 5000 Baltic tellin, around 20,000 sand-hoppers and about 50,000 *Hydrobia* snails. No two species of wading bird have an identical diet, nor do the species feed for the same length of time during a tidal cycle; also, of course, the long-legged waders are able to feed in deeper water than those with shorter legs. Another important factor in the sharing of this abundance of food is the length of a bird's bill: the prey species live at varying depths, so each wading bird exploits different prey according to the length of its bill. All these considerations mean that there is surprisingly little competition for food between one bird and another.

A bird's bill is subject to a lot of wear and tear, but it continues to grow throughout the life of the bird. A European exception to this rule is found in the puffin, whose bill develops brightly coloured plates during the breeding season; these are shed in autumn, leaving the bird with a less attractive but less bulky bill for the winter season.

The oystercatcher does not restrict its diet to oysters, but also feeds on other bivalve molluscs, including cockles, mussels and scallops, as well as gastropods such as limpets and whelks. By day, the oyster-catcher is able to recognize the marks left by cockles on the surface of sand or mud; at night, it pokes its bill just below the surface and walks forward until a cockle is located. The bird then levers the cockle out of hiding with its bill and proceeds to open it by means of powerful blows, again using its bill. The oystercatcher also hunts for cockles and mussels in shallow water, where the animals' shells are slightly ajar so that they can feed; the bird quickly stabs and cuts the adductor muscle, which controls the shell's opening and closing movements, and forces the shells apart with its bill.

Turnstones use their stout bills to turn over stones, seaweed, drift-wood or dead fish in their hunt for insects or small crustaceans; they are also capable of prising limpets and periwinkles from rocks. A bird's bill is its main food-searching organ, and the different shapes have evolved to enable each species to exploit a particular niche. A bill has many highly sensitive cells in its make-up. A wading bird is able to probe into soft earth, sand or mud to detect and grasp food with the tip of the bill, which is both sensitive and flexible.

Winter is a good time for watching wading birds probing for food, for observing their flight patterns and for noting their behaviour. Wading birds and waterfowl have developed routines which take advantage of any opportunity of feeding. The behaviour patterns of shore birds such as turnstones, curlews, oystercatchers, knots and dunlins are controlled by the cycle of the tides. At high tide these birds are forced off their mud-flat feeding grounds, and many gather at the top of the shore to sleep in tightly packed groups until the tide begins to ebb; but when the sea has covered the mid-tide zone, some oystercatchers and curlews fly to coastal pastures, where they join flocks of lapwings and golden plovers. The time of high water changes by roughly an hour each day and the height of the tide varies with the lunar cycle; yet the birds are able to predict accurately the time to leave the farmland, which may be some distance inland, and arrive on their newly exposed strip of mud-flat to resume feeding. Meanwhile, the birds which have been roosting on the upper shore start to feed as soon as the tide begins to ebb, moving down the shore as the sea retreats. The waders with the longest bills, such as the curlews and godwits, leave their roosts later, as their main sources of food – lugworms and ragworms – are found lower down the shore and therefore remain underwater longer.

Wading birds face various problems in winter, when bad weather can make feeding very difficult. Strong winds hamper feeding, as the sand or mud dries out quickly and the invertebrates remain deep in their burrows, not giving away their positions to birds which hunt by sight. A frost may cover the shore with a skin of ice that makes feeding impossible; or it may be so cold that the invertebrates become sluggish and remain inactive under the mud.

WILDFOWL

Availability of food is the primary driving force in moving southwards to overwinter; the freezing of freshwater habitats and soil, or a persistent snow layer, may form a barrier between an animal and its food, so that wading birds and wildfowl must leave their summer breeding grounds in the Arctic regions in order to survive. Ducks, geese and swans leave the far north of Europe in autumn to overwinter in the Danish islands or in Britain and Ireland, swelling the resident populations along the coast and in lakes, rivers, reservoirs and gravel pits. There has to be a great deal of food available for these birds to survive the winter months, but, as with the wading birds, the differences in their preferred habitats and feeding methods ensure that there is little competition between the species.

There are two basic types of duck, the surface-feeding dabblers and the diving ducks. Dabbling ducks have flat, horizontal backs, pointed tails held well up and broad, blunt bills with which they sift food from the water surface. These ducks are largely omnivorous; their bills have horny or rubbery plates, known as lamellae, along their edges. Water is pumped in and out of the duck's mouth and the comb-like plates of the lamellae retain food. The size of the gap between the lamellae varies in relation to the size of the food eaten by the duck; teal and shoveler have very narrow gaps in the plates, as they feed on the tiny seeds of water plants and small freshwater crustaceans. Mallard and pintail, on the other hand, eat a variety of seeds and water animals, so they have wider-spaced lamellae.

The shoveler, gadwall and garganey are dabbling ducks usually found in freshwater habitats, around the edges of lakes or in shallow flood water and marshes, while mallard, teal and pintail can be seen in estuaries as well as in freshwater habitats. The wigeon is the exception among the dabbling ducks; it is a grazing bird with a small bill and may be found eating grass and vegetation from the edges of fresh water and over salt marshes.

Diving ducks are a different shape to dabbling ducks. They have a rounded back and a tail that slopes into the water, while their bills vary in shape according to the food they eat. The goosander, smew and red-breasted merganser have long, narrow bills with saw-like edges for gripping wriggling, slippery fish; the goosander and smew can be found in freshwater lakes, gravel pits and reservoirs, while the red-breasted merganser is also to be seen in coastal waters. Scoters and long-tailed ducks have strong bills with which they crack shellfish, but the eider duck has an even heavier, stronger bill, able to break open shellfish, crabs and sea urchins. These ducks spend most of their lives in coastal waters. Goldeneye, pochard and tufted ducks have short bills; they feed on water vegetation, insect larvae and small crustaceans in freshwater habitats. Diving ducks may feed at the surface, but they usually dive down to catch their food.

During a hard winter, the species feeding in coastal waters will fare better than those of fresh water, which may have to contend with ice-covered habitats where their food is sealed in and made unavailable. Under these circumstances the ducks have to fly in search of food, and in doing so they use up valuable energy resources.

In order to make a non-stop migration flight, ducks, geese and swans, like songbirds, must be well prepared for the journey. Flight muscles must be built up and a layer of fat laid down to use as fuel during the long flight; this is easily done, as a period of plenty comes before the journey begins. Small birds are able to double their weight before migrating, but geese and swans cannot carry such large reserves of fat or they would never become airborne! Geese are able to conserve some of their energy by flying in a V-formation on long journeys. Each bird gets an extra lift from the slipstream of the bird in front and from time to time the leader drops back to allow another

mallard

bird to take on the hard work of being ahead of the others. These large birds fly faster than smaller ones and are less influenced by the wind; nevertheless at the beginning of the season, geese will wait for a favourable wind before starting their migration flight.

Geese and swans are vegetarians. The growing parts of plants in the Arctic breeding grounds contain more protein than those of similar plants in lower latitudes, but grinding plants and releasing their cell sap is an inefficient method of feeding, so geese and swans have to eat vast quantities of food and pass it rapidly through their bodies in order to gain energy. A flock of geese will spend most of the day grazing, and to make the most of a poor diet the birds choose the most succulent green shoots. The white-fronted goose, the Canada goose and the bean goose graze on the grass bordering freshwater habitats, but the barnacle goose enjoys the grass from meadows that have been improved for sheep rearing, often incurring the farmers' wrath.

The pink-footed goose, from Iceland and the east of Greenland, grazes around estuaries and salt marshes, spilling over into arable land, where it enjoys root crops such as carrots; but it is the brent goose which seems to cause most controversy. This dark little sea goose, from the northern tundras of Siberia, used to feed intertidally on estuaries and salt marshes, grazing on eel grass, *Zostera marina*, or on one or two species of algae. However, about twenty years ago, the populations of brent geese began to grow as a result of successful breeding seasons and the bird's removal from the permitted hunting lists of several countries. Each autumn, when the flocks flew south for the winter, there were more and more brent geese visiting the estuaries of Britain, Ireland, Holland, France and Denmark, but the population explosion meant that their rather specialized food became insufficient for their numbers. Rather than starve, the geese began to fly inland to graze on fields of winter wheat and rich pastureland, causing conflict with the farmers. Now 'scaring' techniques are used to frighten the overwintering geese away from crops, and feeding stations have been set up for them instead.

Wild swans, like wild geese, have a romance and distinction that sets them apart. Each October, flocks of swans leave their summer breeding grounds in Iceland and the northern tundras of Siberia to overwinter further south. Whooper swans and Bewick swans join our resident mute swans in shallow estuaries, lowland fields and flooded grasslands; they are occasionally seen in mixed flocks, but usually only

If you examine the muddy area by a pond or stream, you may see the tracks of animals which have been drinking there, or which have left the water to spend some time on land. You may find interesting pieces of plant and animal debris, too.

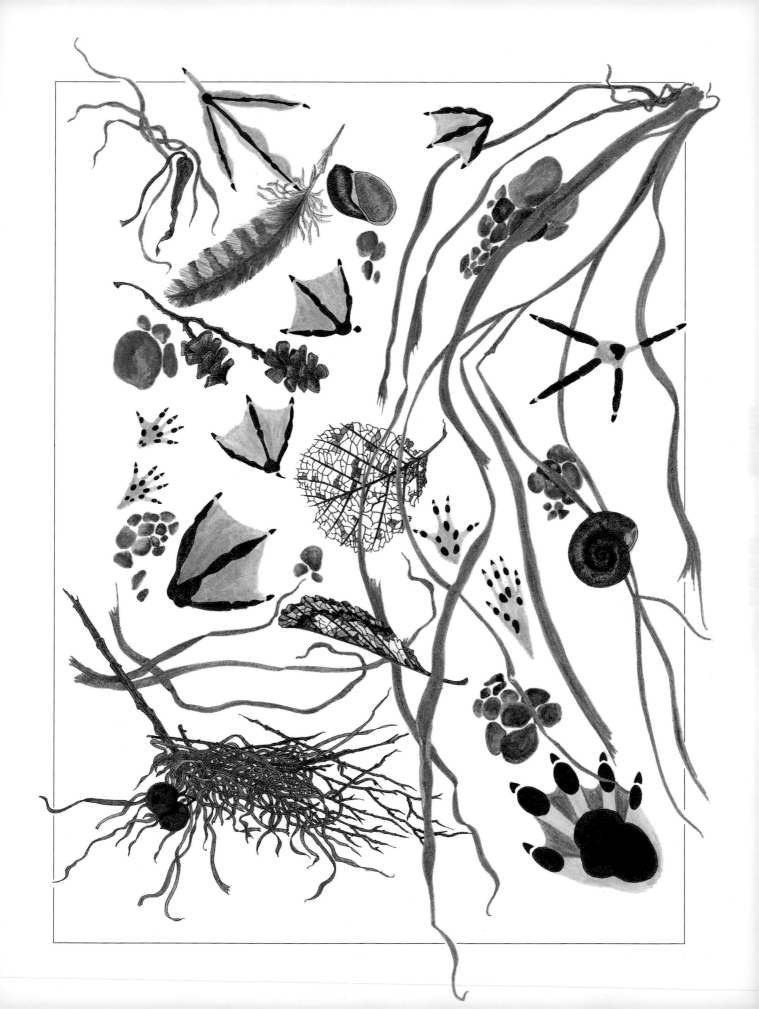

one species is found at a particular locality. The swans feed on water plants and graze on grass; sometimes they visit harvested fields in search of spilt grain and pieces of broken potatoes. Swans are so large and elegant, so purposeful and unhurried as they move with measured steps to graze; occasionally one will look up, neck arched, then extended, a silent warning to the rest of the flock that they are not alone. They are secretive, too, for if their chosen pasture becomes frozen or snow-covered, the swans disappear, to return only when a thaw sets in.

Wading birds and wildfowl are to be seen in flocks in winter. Birds only gather together in this way when there is an advantage to be gained. A solitary bird is much more likely to be killed by a raptor than one that is part of a flock. There are always some birds looking out for danger; the protection of the flock allows more time to be devoted to feeding and this is most important in winter.

FISH IN WINTER

I think that fish must know their own surroundings well, learning about their territory as they move around in search of food, as they follow currents or are guided by water temperatures. So it follows that fish such as cod, bass and herring, which migrate in order to meet their need for breeding grounds, feeding areas or hospitable winter requirements, also know where they are going; for, like birds, they do it every year at the same time and following the same oceanic routes. Migrating fish take advantage of ocean currents in the way that birds and insects use air currents, so as to reduce the amount of effort required to travel to the place, or in the direction, of their choice.

Sea fish are usually less vulnerable than freshwater fish to the effects of severe cold, as the vast ocean retains much of its warmth and rarely becomes as cold as freshwater rivers and lakes; the freezing point of sea water is lower than that of fresh water, as the density is greater. However, in very severe winters, fish migrate *en masse* from inshore waters and estuaries to deeper waters in order to avoid the cold. Sole, which are bottom-living flatfish, are particularly sensitive to cold and they migrate in the autumn from coastal waters to the deeper parts of the southern North Sea, where they spend the winter months. Fish in freshwater habitats also leave shallow waters when they begin to feel the cold, to congregate in pools or to move downstream in search of deeper water. But throughout the winter months freshwater fish usually become less active, feeding less and lying low in the water.

It seems strange, then, that salmon and trout should spawn in winter, when the water in the upper reaches of rivers is very cold. The ability of the salmon and the sea trout once more to find the mouth of the river that they left four years earlier is amazing. When the two-year-old fish left the river, it knew the smell, tastes and features of its home area very well; and while growing up in the sea it carries the memory of its native waters with it. The longer the river is, the earlier the fish must enter it to reach the spawning grounds, with their beds of silt-free gravel and well-oxygenated water.

Males and females gather and by November spawning starts. The female makes a well-defined, saucer-shaped depression in the gravel, using her tail. Some of the gravel is carried away, but much of it forms a mound on the downstream edge of the nest, or redd, that she is making. While this is happening, the male is protecting the female from the attentions of other males; so when the female crouches in the redd to lay her eggs, he is on hand, ready to shed his milt over them so that they will be fertilized. The female covers the eggs with gravel by flicking the mound at the side of the redd with her tail.

Throughout the winter months the large, yolk-filled eggs lie under 15 cm (6 in) or so of gravel, and at the end of January the fish embryos begin to develop, their growth rate depending on the temperature of the water. Many of the parent fish die of starvation, disease or exhaustion, but the strongest swim back to the sea to regain their health and vigour. Brown trout and rainbow trout lay their eggs in winter, too, but these fish do not migrate to the sea; instead they jealously guard good positions or 'lies' in the river, the most dominant fish having the best 'lie' of all.

PLAYFUL OTTERS

The otter, stoat, weasel, pine marten, polecat and mink are all members of the weasel family, Mustelidae. Otters are found in many parts of the world; the two best known species are the common or European otter and the Canadian otter. The European otter's range extends from the British Isles across Russia to Japan; it is also found in North America. The Canadian or river otter is found throughout the United States and in all but the far north of Canada.

Otters are land animals that spend much of their time in water. They are adapted to life in a watery environment and they also cope well with the cold of winter. The otter's long body, with its small head, thick neck and rudder-like tail, is designed for moving fast both in water and on land. The otter has large lungs, enabling it to breathe in enough air to keep it going for three or four minutes under water; during this time it can swim up to 400 metres ($^1/_4$ mile) to escape from danger, or to catch a fish. Other features are adapted to support the otter's underwater hunting and swimming abilities. Its ears project little beyond its thick fur, so retaining the streamlined body shape. When submerged the ears and nostrils are closed by special valves;

muscles around the eyes adjust the focus, to correct distorted vision caused by the water. Bunches of stiff facial whiskers are sensitive to the vibrations of other animals, so helping the otter to catch prey when in dark water; the five toes on each foot are webbed, like those of a duck, to give speed and strength in swimming.

The otter's coat is both warm and waterproof. The thick fur is in two layers: the outer layer is of long, coarse guard hairs which bunch together in groups when the coat is wet, making the otter look spiky; the under fur is very fine and so thick that, when the otter is underwater, the hairs trap a layer of air which insulates the animal and prevents water from reaching the skin. This layer of air gives the otter a silvery appearance when it swims, while a trail of bubbles marks its progress through the water. The otter spends a lot of time grooming and caring for its valuable, protective coat.

Otters are protected by law in Britain; but they are vulnerable to the pesticides which drain into their habitat, polluting the water and contaminating fish. Often the fish remain unaffected by the small amounts of poison they ingest, but the poison contained within their bodies accumulates and becomes a lethal dose within the body of an otter, which eats many fish. Detergents in the water can destroy the otter's fur coat, and when the animal is unable to resist wet and cold it succumbs to both and dies. In addition, each otter needs a territory of 20–30 km (12–18 miles) of undisturbed waterside, backed by some quiet countryside, so that it will not exhaust the food supply of a particular area. This is difficult when many habitats have been altered by building work, drainage schemes and intensive farming methods; the waterways themselves are often disturbed by water sports of various kinds, all of which are offputting to otters. Because of the pressures on the countryside, otters in Britain are few and far between; their last stronghold is probably in the Highlands and Islands of Scotland. In the other countries where the European otter is found, there are larger tracts of uninhabited countryside where these animals can live their private lives in peace.

During the harsh winters among the snow-covered glens and mountains, where the temperatures are usually below freezing point, the otter is kept snug in its warm pelage. A major problem is a shortage of food, because, as we have seen, prey such as freshwater crayfish, eels and frogs overwinter in deep mud or in narrow crevices, in a state of inactivity, while shoals of fish overwinter in deep water where they are less vulnerable to cold. So in winter the otter often hunts for water voles, or swims under waterfowl to drag them down and drown them; as a last resort it will also eat carrion. When the water in the habitat is frozen, the otter looks for relatively thin patches and claws at the ice, eventually digging a way through it, in order to enter the water beneath. An otter may make many holes in the ice this way, and is then able to relocate them from under the water. If it is not too far from the sea, an otter will migrate to the coast to avoid severe weather; there it is able to find more food and slightly warmer temperatures. But the otter cannot swim in heavy seas and has to rely on hunting along the tide line in times of stormy weather. Otters which remain inland in winter also have the hazard of storms to contend with. Heavy rain may increase the volume of a river, so that it runs in a flood, or spate, with enormous power; the otter is unable to swim or hunt in water that is flowing so fast.

Otters usually live alone, moving around by night; during the day they rest in dens often known as hovers, which are well hidden under tree roots or in dense vegetation. The breeding den is called a holt and this is where the dog and bitch live together for a few weeks before the female drives the male away and the cubs are born. The well-hidden holt must be situated above the level of winter floods, and far enough away from the water's edge for the mother otter to be sure that the cubs will not fall in and drown before they are old enough to swim. In Britain, otter cubs may be born during any month of the year, while in the northernmost parts of their range, the same species of otter only gives birth in spring and summer.

Otters are playful animals. A mother otter will play with her cubs, adult pairs will play together and even solitary otters enjoy playing with pebbles or swimming on their backs and rolling around in the water, apparently just for fun. Otter cubs stay with their mother for up to a year, learning to hunt and look after themselves; they often have fun as a family sliding down snow-covered or muddy banks into water, then climbing up the slope to do it again and again. Once, many years ago, I was fortunate enough to see an otter family playing in this way and, more recently in America, I have seen another species of otter playing the same games on the muddy bank of a lake.

In some ways winter in a watery habitat seems to offer rather more comfort than overwintering on dry land – it is warmer and contains a lot of food for some animals. But the water that drains into freshwater habitats from farmland that has been extensively fertilized, or sprayed with pesticides, joins with contaminated water from industrial sites to pollute the waterways. Rivers carry this pollution to the sea, poisoning the estuaries and the ocean, where nuclear power stations and the dumping of various wastes add to the toxicity. Many creatures are well adapted for the harshness of winter, but how long will animals that have to live amidst our waste products survive?

THE COUNTRYSIDE IN WINTER

A glimpse of a scarlet berry or the sparkle of a frosted spider's web gives unexpected pleasure when the bleak winter season grips the land. Take time to wander through this muffled, mystical world where the laws of nature seem to have been suspended.

TREES IN WINTER

The silhouettes of trees are conspicuous features in a winter landscape. Standing naked, their green mantles shed, the details of their basic branching patterns may be seen etched clearly against the sky.

Trees have thick, straight trunks which rise for some distance above the ground before dividing into several branches, which in turn branch again and again. The tapering shape of a tree trunk, with the widest part at the base, enables the tree to resist the force of the wind; tall chimneys are built in this shape for the same reason. The larger a plant is, the more vulnerable it is to the physical forces of wind, rain, snow and gravity; trees overcome the problem by producing tissues which provide great strength. Every cell in the roots, trunk and branches of a tree has specially thickened walls; when these cells die, they become lignified – that is, they perform the vital function of forming wood. Bark, the hard, corky outer layer of trees and shrubs, cannot stretch; so, as the tree grows and expands, the outer tissues crack in characteristic patterns. In some trees, such as the plane, the outer layer of bark strips off; in birches it peels in thin strips, while the bark of other trees, such as oak or elm, becomes deeply fissured. In response to this natural wounding, a waterproof layer is formed to protect the tissues within the tree trunk.

Branches and twigs are also thick at their base and narrow towards their apex. Trees vary in their degree of branching; most trees of temperate climates branch again and again to produce large numbers of slender twigs which, in their turn, carry many leaves in summer. In warmer climates, with high humidity, trees usually branch less and have thicker twigs, which carry fewer but larger leaves. The angle at which a branch grows away from the main trunk is important, as are the angles of the smaller branches and twigs. Research shows that a branching angle of 90° requires the least amount of materials in its construction, and that the flow of food and water in the plumbing system of the tree is most efficient when branches in the pipeline are at

According to folklore, when holly, ivy and mistletoe are twined together into a circle, their protective properties are very strong.

right angles. Yet there are trees, such as the Lombardy poplar, that have an upright or fastigiate habit; then there are weeping trees, including weeping willow and weeping ash, whose branches grow so fast that the trunk cannot bear the weight and so the branches spread wide and droop down.

mistletoe

The overall shape of a tree is determined by its species; but even in a single species differences in form can be produced by varying the planting distances, by positioning, by wind action or by pruning. A tree which stands alone often retains branches low down on the developing trunk; such a tree carries a summer canopy of foliage sweeping from the top of the crown to the ground. Trees growing close together, on the other hand, lose their lower branches as a result of shading. In an area where cattle graze, trees are cropped to the height which the animals are able to reach, while those grown in gardens are usually pruned and trained as they develop. A tree which is partly shaded by a building may grow lopsided, the side which is fully in the light being stronger than the shaded side.

The effect of weather can also determine the shape of a tree. Branches may be broken by wind or by lightning and, in coastal areas, prevailing winds often cause trees to develop on the leeward side only, so that trees in this situation may be stunted. Look out, too, for trees that have been shaped by man. A tree which has been coppiced – that is, cut back to its base – can be identified by the number of trunks or stems that rise from a single root base. New shoots grow from the stump, or stool, of coppiced trees, and after a few years these can be used as fence poles, or put to other uses. Some trees, such as willow, hornbeam and beech, may be pollarded; this is a method of cutting the tree back to a single upright bole every few years. The trees are 'beheaded' by having their branches hewn back and the trunk cut to within 2 metres (6 ft) of the ground. This encourages the tree to throw up new branches, for poles or firewood, well out of reach of grazing and browsing animals.

Winter is a good time to take a closer look at the twigs of deciduous trees, which often give colour to the landscape at this time of year. Dogwood has red twigs; those of beech and oak are a rich purple-brown; ash twigs are a soft grey. The leaf buds of each species also vary in size, shape and colour: ash twigs have angular black buds; beeches have long, pointed, light brown buds; alder buds are purplish, while the hazel has small, green, globular buds on zigzag twigs. Leaves do not grow on a stem in a haphazard manner; they arise with mathematical precision at definite and regular intervals. The arrangement of leaves on a stem is known as phyllotaxy, meaning 'leaf order'. The leaf buds of sycamore, horse chestnut and honeysuckle are in opposite pairs; those of beech, hornbeam, hazel and elm are arranged on either side of the stem in two ranks, but not in opposite pairs; buckthorns, poplars and plants in the rose family have leaf buds arranged in a spiral around the twig.

Look at twigs from different species of trees: the thicker the twig the larger the leaf bud and the larger the leaf will be when it opens. The horse chestnut, for example, has thick twigs and large, sticky, red-brown leaf buds. You may also notice that some trees already carry flower buds. These are tightly closed against the frosts and winds, but they will quickly open when the day length increases and the sun becomes warm. You will probably find grey-green hazel catkins, the fat, brown flower buds of elm, the fat, shiny, pointed flower buds of aspen and the immature male catkins of alder alongside the small female flower buds.

FUNGUS SPOTTING

On a winter's walk you may spot the remains of autumn fungi, become aware of the perennial species or see some of the few that favour colder conditions.

Fungi are strange plants. Many are minute, only visible to the naked eye as cotton-like threads in the compost heap or in rotting wood, while some form blue-green moulds on stale bread and other old food. Autumn is the favoured time for mushrooms and toadstools to raise their fruiting bodies, as if by magic, in grassland, woodland and along the hedgerows.

Fungi, together with bacteria, are decomposers and as such are as important to the environment, as are green plants, the producers. Fungi have no chlorophyll, so they are unable to manufacture their own food; instead, they utilize the organic materials produced by other plants and animals. They do this in several ways: they may feed on dead or decaying organisms, such as a dead animal, a dead branch or fallen leaves; or they may live as parasites, taking the nutrients they require from living plants or animals, to the detriment of the host body. Some are parasitic only until the host dies, when the fungus becomes saprophytic and feeds on the dead organism; honey fungus, *Armillaria mellea*, falls into this category. Other fungi grow in harmony with plants that may be living in soils deficient in nitrogen. In this type of relationship, fungal threads, or hyphae, penetrate the roots of the green plant and an exchange of nutrients takes place; the fungus takes sugars from the green plant and in return passes nitrogen, taken from decaying matter, to the green plant. This partnership is called symbiosis or mutualism. Many trees, orchids, heaths and heathers could not grow properly, or at all, without a fungal associate.

Autumn is the best time to see mushrooms and toadstools of different shapes, sizes and colours, but there is an opportunity to see other

hazel

kinds of fungi when winter comes along, the trees are bare of leaves and there are few or no flowers to distract the attention.

There is a dainty fungus called 'little hoods', *Mycena corticola*, which grows among the moss on the bark of deciduous trees. Its little grey-pink, grooved bells or bonnets are borne on slender stems, about 1 cm (less than $^1/_2$ in) high, with short, stiff hairs at the base. Coral spot, *Nectria cinnabarina*, is common at all times of the year, but its cheerful vermilion-red cushions, bursting through the bark of fallen branches and twigs, draw the attention in winter. Look on dead or dying deciduous trees for the hard, round fungus called King Alfred's cakes, *Daldinia concentrica*, dark chocolate brown when it is young, but black and shiny when fully grown. A remarkable feature of this plant is that the fruiting body contains its own store of water, enabling it to disperse its spores during dry spells; it even continues to do so when it is taken into a dry room in a house. Folklore tells us that it cures night cramps if placed at the bottom of the bed.

The jade green cups of *Chlorociboria aeruginascens* may be seen on rotting logs and branches, especially of oak. The fungus stains the wood an attractive bright blue-green and the naturally coloured wood was once used to inlay snuff boxes and jewel caskets. This interesting craft work was carried out, until the late nineteenth century, in Tonbridge, Kent, and became known as 'Tonbridge Ware'. Scarlet elf cups, *Sarcoscypha coccinea*, are round cups 2–5 cm (1–2 in) in diameter; the inner scarlet surface is smooth, while the outer surface is white, with a thick coat of matted hairs. This fungus is most abundant in winter, when it may be seen on fallen, decaying branches in damp woodlands. The bright yellow-orange, jelly-like fruiting body of *Tremella mesenterica*, golden jelly, is found in similar wet woodland conditions.

Fallen timber and dead, dying or living trees often bear the horizontal growths of bracket fungi. These are usually fan-shaped or semi-circular; most emerge directly from the wood upon which they are living, while others may be attached by a short, thick stem. The underside of the fungus usually has gills or tubes, from which the spores are dispersed. Some of the bracket fungi are annual and decompose after shedding their spores; others are perennial and continue to grow in size for a number of years, producing a new crop of spores every year. These perennial fungi are tough and have a leathery or woody texture; if they are cut downwards, the annual production of tissues can be seen in layers through the fruiting body, rather like the growth rings on a tree stump.

Panellus stipticus is a bracket fungus; light brown in colour, it normally looks like many other such fungi, but when it is moist and actively growing it glows in the dark, creating a surprising effect. It is interesting to look closely at bracket fungi; to compare their textures, which may be hard and leathery or soft and velvety; to see how they disperse their spores, by gills or by tubes; and to look at their colours, which may be sombre or strikingly beautiful in the half-light of winter.

OCCASIONAL FLOWERS

It is quite a challenge to find flowers in the countryside in winter, but one or two do linger on. You may see a late scarlet pimpernel scrambling on a roadside verge, a froth of creamy hogweed or a red-stemmed herb robert. Ivy is the last flower to bloom in the year, offering nectar to insects with short tongues, especially flies; if the weather is sunny, a few late wasps may also collect around the glistening globular heads of greenish-yellow flowers.

Gorse, *Ulex europaeus*, is a prickly evergreen shrub of the pea family. It often flaunts its bright yellow flowers during the bleak days of winter. This is a very resilient plant with thick, thorn-like foliage; it flowers almost all year round, deterred only by spells of hard frost – hence the old country saying, 'When the gorse is out of bloom, kissing is out of season.' In spring the sharp foliage gives protection to the nests of birds such as whinchats, stonechats, linnets and the rare Dartford warbler, while at the same time the plant guards itself against herbivores which may try to eat it. Before coal was put into use for fires, gorse was valued as a fuel when wood was scarce; it was cut and tied into bundles to be burnt in ovens and kilns. It was also crushed and used as winter food for livestock.

Butcher's broom, *Ruscus aculeatus*, is another spiky evergreen, but it belongs, surprisingly, to the lily family. It grows in dry woodlands and looks as if it has broad, flattened leaves which end in a spike; however, when its little green flowers open, during the autumn or winter, they can be seen to be in the centre of the 'leaves'. A leaf would never bear a flower in this way and the leaf-like structures of butcher's broom are really flattened branches called cladodes; the true leaves of the plant are reduced to tiny scales. The flowers on the female plants are followed by large red berries which are both beautiful and distinctive, sitting in the middle of a green 'leaf'. The plant has been given its common name because butchers once used the stiff shoots for sweeping their chopping blocks.

Stinking hellebore, *Helleborus foetidus*, is a plant of limestone areas that opens its purple-tipped green flowers even when snow is about. The scent of the flower and the smell of the foliage when crushed are disagreeable, hence the plant's common name. The Christmas rose, *Helleborus niger*, is a short-stemmed, white hellebore widely grown in gardens, which brings cheer during the shortest days of the year.

Look at the flowers of hellebores carefully. The structures we immediately think of as petals are really the sepals of the flower, the true petals being modified into small tubes with jagged rims that act as nectaries. These two species of hellebore flower from December to March and are visited by the few longer-tongued insects that may be about, and feeling very hungry, on sunny winter days.

DISTINCTIVE DEAD HEADS

Herbaceous plants die down in winter, but many of them produce summer-flowering stems that are so strengthened that they do not collapse when they die. Instead, they remain standing throughout the winter in groups which provide interesting shapes and colours in an otherwise barren scene.

The red-brown stems of docks are distinctive; the remains of flowers and fruits usually decorate them. Red and white campion have straw-coloured stems in winter, with the remains of flask-shaped fruiting capsules. Plants of St John's wort have wiry, dark brown stems carrying the remains of seed capsules, while willowherbs stand tall, with dead leaves hanging and seed pods split and empty at the tops of the stems. I look forward to seeing umbellifers such as hogweed on my winter walks. They are among the most distinctive of all the dead heads: the stems are hollow and often ribbed, providing hiding places for small invertebrates, while the flat-topped heads retain the rays of the umbels that give the family its name.

Great mullein and foxgloves also stand tall, with dark, empty seed capsules persisting. Bracken branches droop, their beautiful tawny fronds dry and brittle now, but giving so much colour in the grey light. One of the unmistakable winter dead heads is the teasel, its spiny oval heads now mouse brown atop tough, spiny stems; lesser burdock plants are almost tree-like in shape, while tall, spiky thistles hold their straw-coloured heads high. In marshy areas reedmace raises its brown velvet seed heads, topped by a thin stalk which once carried the male flowers; tall reeds sway in the wind, making a sound like a gentle sea; and purple loosestrife is very persistent with whorls of withered flowers. Bleached grass stems are to be seen everywhere and some, such as cock's foot, still bear their empty seed heads.

On my walks I often see goldfinches exploring the dead heads, searching for any seeds that may still be found in them. Through the autumn, family groups of these colourful birds hang on to thistle heads, burdocks and hardheads, swinging to and fro as they probe for seeds with their substantial but finely pointed bills. Goldfinches frequent gardens, allotments, wasteland, farmland, scrubland, sand dunes, salt marshes and roadside verges; when they are disturbed they rise, twittering, the liquid notes of their calls sounding like a chime of tiny bells – no wonder the collective noun for goldfinches is 'charm'. A goldfinch's bill enables it to extract seeds from deep inside the heads of teasel; if you examine a teasel head you will see that this operation needs an expert technician to carry it out. Watch carefully and you will see how a goldfinch pulls the seed head forward and clamps the stem down firmly under its feet, in order to extract seeds from the head. Thistles are the favourite food of goldfinches; they eat the seeds from these and other plants through until late autumn. Then they begin to concentrate on fallen seeds on the ground and the seeds of low-growing plants, leaving the seed heads on taller stems for later in the winter, when snow might cover the ground and the shorter-stemmed plants.

goldfinch

Wandering parties of tits work their way along the hedgerow and woodland edge and forage among the old alders on the riverside. These groups of nomads roam over a large area, but they appear to have a daily routine or pattern; the flocks are mainly composed of blue tits and great tits, but there are also marsh tits, coal tits and treecreepers. They call to each other constantly, keeping the wanderers together in their search for food. Foraging in this way increases the possibility of finding good food sources, and the many pairs of eyes are more likely to spot a predator in the offing.

Troupes of long-tailed tits are a special treat to see. They are so acrobatic and agile as they move quickly from tree to tree and bush to bush in their search for insects and spiders, winkling the hibernating invertebrates out from crevices with their narrow, pointed beaks. Long-tailed tits are so small that they lose heat quickly and have diffi-culty in keeping warm in winter when food is scarce; consequently many die in severe weather.

THE SEARCH FOR FOOD

When blackberries, rowan and elderberries have all been eaten and the November winds come roaring from the north-east, driving worms deep into the ground and other invertebrates into hiding, the hard-ships of a bird's life begin in earnest.

Hedgerows and farmland appear to be bleak and empty, but if you stand still and watch quietly you will soon discover that there is con-stant activity at the edge of the fields and in the shelter of the hedgerows. A mature hedge makes a particularly rich habitat as it often forms an extension to a nearby wood or copse; it gives protection and cover to plants, birds and other animals from the open fields, while having its own particular species living in its shelter. Many birds roost in hedges, where the tangle of twigs offers some shelter from bad weather – especially from the cold wind, which causes great loss of heat and energy during the long hours of winter darkness. The wilder, unmanaged hedgerows that have been allowed to mature provide a relatively safe route by which animals are able to travel from one habitat to another. These hedgerows often radiate out from woodlands and extend the woodland food supply in a long, narrow corridor. So squirrels living in the wood spread their search for hazelnuts along the hedgerows; foxes and stoats use the hedgerow to stalk prey; badgers root along the bottom of the hedge for whatever they can find; and insects hibernate among the stems of the many plants. There is a wide range of food in a mature hedgerow highway, where the plant community interlaces to make it a very attractive winter habitat.

Large numbers of fieldfares and redwings fly southwards to share any rosehips, holly, sloe and hawthorn berries with thrushes and blackbirds. During my winter walks I often see flocks of fieldfares and redwings feeding on farmland and playing fields; but very cold weather sends them into gardens, where fallen apples and pears, any remaining berries and the food on the bird table are all eaten up before the flock moves on. When freezing conditions are prolonged, the birds are forced to fly further south, but the weaker ones do not survive.

Birds must work very hard to find enough food to keep them alive during the winter months. There is such a short day in which to search, just a few hours of daylight, then the long, cold night; so a bird must hunt quickly and carefully, always being aware that it may be being hunted itself. Walking through a wood, or in the park, you may have heard the sound of fallen leaves being turned over as a bird searches for any invertebrate that may be hiding there. Have you ever put yourself in the position of a bird trying to find food in winter? It is an interesting test and will make you more aware of the difficulties of winter survival. On hands and

goldfinch

knees in a cold wood or in the garden, you may carefully turn over leaf after leaf but only find one or two nuts, a tiny snail and a half-frozen worm in a quarter of an hour – which should give pause for thought. The problems are multiplied when snow covers the ground; but we human animals can help the birds that visit our gardens.

Some people say that it is wrong to feed birds, as it interferes with nature; but the provision of a little food and water is surely scant return for the hedge-cutting that is done too early and the habitats that are destroyed in the name of progress. You can feed birds simply by throwing crusts of stale bread outside; but this method is full of danger, as the message goes around the local cat community and they home in on the feeding birds. There are a number of bird-feeding devices on the market that can be put in safe places and will suit all kinds of situations. There are open bird tables, covered bird tables, baskets to hold kitchen scraps, seed hoppers, nut holders and other ingenious inventions. Some of these are adaptable, so that even if you don't have a garden, you should be able to fasten a feeder of some sort to a windowsill.

Birds need carbohydrates and fat to help them build up the energy reserves needed to survive long winter nights. Many kitchen scraps, such as cooked suet, bacon rind and marrow bone are good value; as are pieces of stale cheese, meat fat and pastry. Cut open cooked potatoes in their jackets; give cooked spaghetti and cooked rice; but **never** give birds uncooked rice or desiccated coconut, as these will swell up inside the bird's stomach, often with fatal results. Birds enjoy bread dampened with water or bacon fat, stale cake crumbs and the bits from the bottom of the biscuit tin. Try them with pieces of apple and pear, soaked dried fruits, unsalted peanuts and other sorts of nuts, including half-coconuts; these are all nourishing, while seeds of every kind, besides providing carbohydrates and fats, also contain oils, minerals and vitamins. We are vegetarians, so we don't use any of the meat-associated foods that birds enjoy, but we have found that tins of cat food are beneficial to birds and hedgehogs alike. Do **not** feed birds with highly seasoned or well-salted food, but please **do** give them water. They need it to drink and for bathing; bathing is always followed by preening, and preening maintains the insulating properties of feathers, keeping them oiled and in good condition.

Having loaded the bird table, sit back and watch. You will see that each species of bird behaves in a different way and likes different things to eat. Tits perform acrobatics on suspended half-coconuts and strings of peanuts; nuthatches take nuts away to jam them into a crevice in order to eat them; sparrows dunk bread into water before eating it, while thrushes and blackbirds tackle the fruit. It is worthwhile to crumble cheese very finely and sprinkle it amongst the leaf litter in the lee of a hedge where wrens, which do not visit bird tables, will find it. Dunnocks do not venture on to a feeding station either; instead they wait for food to fall to the ground, so scattering a little food would make their day.

Robins defend a territory throughout the winter and so you will only have one robin visiting your bird table; should another appear, watch the feathers fly. Greenfinches have a taste for sunflower seeds and can be very selfish when feeding on them; if another greenfinch arrives to share the feast, the one which was at the table first will often spread its wings and scream at the newcomer, trying to send it away by blustering. But a continuous stream of tits and finches will share the pickings with other birds; it is interesting to see the numbers and species that a bird table encourages to visit. We changed our bird table from an open one to a covered one because pheasants flew on to the open one and wouldn't allow any other birds to come for food! Great spotted woodpeckers visit, and nuthatches queue up for nuts; one day, much to my amazement, a kestrel swooped down and carried a blue tit off. Well, that's nature.

SLEEPING TOGETHER

When birds roost communally they are able to conserve energy by snuggling together and keeping each other warm. A solitary bird roosting in an exposed place on a cold winter's night may freeze to death, or be caught by a predator; a number of birds all huddled together keep warmer and enjoy the safety of numbers. As I have mentioned before, many wrens cram themselves into nest boxes in order to warm each other and beat the cold; blue tits and great tits also sleep in groups in the crevices of trees or buildings, avoiding draughts and preventing heat loss. Quails roost in clusters, too, all with their heads pointing outwards, ready to sound the alarm and disperse if danger threatens.

Crows, magpies and ravens roost communally in quite large numbers outside the breeding season; rooks, of course, live in communities, making a spectacular sight weaving to and fro in the air before settling down for the night. But the birds I love to watch on a winter afternoon are starlings. They stop feeding about an hour before dark and set out for their roost. Our house is on the side of a hill overlooking a valley, and it is awe-inspiring to stand and watch the sky fill with flock after flock of countless numbers of starlings. They roost in reed beds and woodlands, but before they go to sleep they carry out a wonderful aerial display, wheeling and ebbing, merging and spreading, rocketing upwards and funnelling downwards; flocks integrate and separate as they sweep back and forth in changing patterns before gradually beginning to swoop down to their own roosting sites. Similar aerobatics take place over cities, too, where anything up to a million birds shelter from the rain and wind on ledges, sills, eaves and cornices.

Each bird has its own particular place to sleep, whether it is clinging to a reed stem, balancing on a twig or sitting on a ledge; it roosts shoulder to shoulder with its neighbour, joining in an evening chorus until darkness falls and the birds sleep. It always amazes me that birds do not fall from their perches when asleep; the explanation is that most perching birds have three toes that face forwards and one backwards, the tendons in the feet and legs being so arranged that when the bird relaxes, its grip tightens.

FAMILIES IN WINTER

It seems strange that when so many birds are fighting for winter survival, with little food and such difficulty in keeping warm, some should choose winter as the season to raise their families. Crossbills, the most specialized of the finches, raise their young between January and March; this is the time when conifer seeds are in good supply, before they have fallen to the ground. Scottish and parrot crossbills have the largest mandibles and they eat pine seeds; common crossbills feed on spruce, while the smaller two-barred crossbills feed on the seeds of larch.

Young birds are usually fed on easily digested insects which are rich in protein; but young crossbills eat few insects, their main food item being a paste of partially digested conifer seeds mixed with mucus regurgitated by the adult. This diet is less nutritious than one of insects, and so the baby crossbills develop at a slower rate than most other birds; they take up to a week longer to fledge than other finches and are dependent on their parents for about six weeks. Because crossbills have such a specialized diet, they have to be prepared to travel when cone crops in a particular area fail; so they tend to be nomadic, moving wherever there is the prospect of food to be gathered.

FAMILY PLANNING

Badgers are found in many countries, the animal known as the European badger having a range extending from the British Isles throughout Europe – apart from the far north – into Japan and southern

goldcrest

China. The American badger is found from south-western Canada to central Mexico. The two species have a similar life-cycle.

Badgers give birth to their young following a period of prolonged inactivity in winter. In Britain, this usually occurs during January or early February: it may be a little earlier in the south, while in the north and east it may be a little later. Up to five youngsters are born; they are blind and helpless and they snuggle together in the deep bed of straw, hay, bracken and dead leaves which makes up their cosy nest. It is important that the nursery chamber in the badgers' sett is well furnished with large quantities of insulating material, as this helps the cubs to retain their body heat, particularly when their mother has left them alone while she forages for food to maintain her own strength and keep up her milk supply.

A few weeks after the cubs are born, the badger sow mates again. She may do so several times throughout the following summer, but February seems to be the peak time for sexual excitement. But instead of the blastocysts – developing eggs – being promptly implanted in the wall of the uterus, they remain free in the womb until the following November or December, when the womb lining becomes receptive. When the eggs do become embedded, they begin to grow rapidly, a placenta is formed and the foetuses are linked to the mother's blood supply which carries food and oxygen to the developing cubs.

Badgers eat a great deal of food in autumn, then they sleep for long periods, remaining in a state of semi-dormancy for several weeks. It is thought that during this time hormones are released which trigger the lining of the womb into becoming receptive. It is probably the same mechanism that induces the brown bear to become receptive to her fertilized egg cells. Brown bears mate in early summer, and after mating the pair part. There is a delayed implantation of the embryos and the cubs are not born until the following January or February, when the female is passing the winter in her cosy den.

The number of cubs born to a brown bear depends on the age of the mother. Comparatively young females, five or six years of age, will only have one cub; mature females have two cubs, while ageing females have either one or two. The newborn cub is very small, weighing less than 450 g (1 lb) and only measuring about 23 cm (9 in) in length. It is blind and toothless and has pale, sparse fur. This diminutive size is probably an adaptation to ensure that the mother bear, who is in a lethargic condition and living on her fat reserves, does not become too exhausted by giving birth or by suckling her young. The female brown bear is a very good mother: she tends to her baby with

Some animals hibernate in winter, while many others have to spend every minute of the short, bleak days hunting for food.

care and affection, licking it incessantly and holding it against the thick fur of her chest to keep it warm. An old legend says that bear cubs are born in a shapeless mass and licked into shape by their mother; hence the expression 'to lick into shape', meaning to train or put into order. The mother bear cares for her young in the den for three months, by which time spring is well established and it is time for the cubs to be weaned.

There are other examples of delayed implantation: roe deer mate in late July and August, but implantation does not occur until December; the young are born in May or June. Seals mate shortly after giving birth, but again there is a delay in implantation and it is a year before another litter is born. The grey seal, which lives on both sides of the North Atlantic, is found on the shores of the Gulf of St Lawrence and Newfoundland, on the eastern side of Iceland, around the British coasts where there are rocky places, along the Norwegian coast and in the Baltic. The pups are born at different times according to the locality of the colony, but always during late autumn and winter.

Although stoats and weasels are similar in many ways, their breeding behaviour is very different. In areas where food is plentiful, weasels may have two or three families during spring and summer; stoats, on the other hand, mate in summer but, due to delayed implantation, the kittens are not born until the following spring.

Some bats, such as the horseshoe and pipistrelle, have delayed fertilization: the females receive sperm from the males in autumn and store it in the vagina or uterus throughout the months of hibernation. When the animals become active again in spring, egg cells are released from the ovary and fertilized by the stored sperm.

Delayed implantation and fertilization must have some advantage for these species. Maybe in some cases it is a compromise between the most convenient time of year for the sexes to meet and the best season for raising the young; or maybe it ensures the continuity of the species should any disaster occur among the males during a severe winter.

Rabbits are notoriously speedy and successful in the art of breeding, the majority of their young being born during the first half of the year. Buck rabbits become sexually mature from December onwards, but the sex organs of the does do not develop until the middle of January; from then on, mating stimulates ovulation. In spite of this, the number of litters produced early in the year is not as high as one might expect, as a large proportion of the embryos break down in the womb and are resorbed into the mother's tissues. This is a rapid process; the embryos and the embryonic and placental tissues shrivel and are resorbed within two or three days. Nevertheless the female then begins to lactate, comes into oestrus and mates as if she had actually given birth to the young.

Resorption is an energy-conserving process and a form of birth control which limits the population when the food supply or available territory may be stretched. So, if snow or extreme weather conditions persist in winter and female rabbits are not able to eat enough food to feed themselves and their unborn young, they resorb their litter and keep up their strength.

COURTSHIP AND UNION

Red foxes are solitary animals for much of the year, but when they carry out their courtship during January and February, the high-pitched calls and screams of their love songs echo unforgettably through the frosty air.

During the mating season, a dog fox may hunt with the vixen of his choice, searching for voles, mice, rats, rabbits, hares and birds. The red fox, like the badger, eats large quantities of insects and earthworms; opportunist feeders of this sort prey on anything they can catch and this flexible diet allows foxes to thrive in unlikely environments. They are often seen in suburbs, and increasingly in city centres, where they raid dustbins and consume anything remotely edible. Walking with a light, almost soundless tread the fox travels long distances, usually by night, hunting for food; in winter snowy tracks often reveal just how far it has travelled.

Popular tradition portrays the fox as a ruthless hunter, capable of killing far more animals than it can eat. There is some truth in this belief: when a fox gets into a situation where there is a lot of prey that cannot escape – such as a hen house – it will often kill every bird. The reason for this is that the fox's killing instincts are triggered by move-ment. In the wild, if a group of animals is attacked, many will scatter and most will escape; then when the victim lies dead and still, the fox is satisfied. But in the confines of a hen house the birds cannot escape and their terrified fluttering stimulates the fox into killing again and again; not for sport, but as a response to the instinct to kill prey whenever the opportunity arises. If a fox did not do this in the wild, it would soon starve.

It was once thought that red and grey squirrels hibernated through the winter, but this is not so, both species being active during many of the short winter days. Squirrels stay curled up in their warm nests, known as dreys, when the weather is very cold, wet or windy, and when there is deep snow or icy conditions; however, they are

Christmas rose

only able to go without food for two or three days, after which time they leave the drey to forage even in severe weather. This is where their secret hoards come in useful – if the squirrels can remember the hiding-places they chose in the autumn!

Grey squirrels live mainly in broad-leaved woodlands and it is easy to spot their dreys high in the trees; they are usually built away from the trunk, balanced in a fork or between thick branches. The dreys of both grey and red squirrels are rounded, about the size of a football, with a side entrance; they are made of close-knit twigs and the pliant stems of ivy and honeysuckle, and lined with leaves and moss. In winter the grey squirrel's coat is thick; it is yellow-brown on the head and flanks and silver-grey elsewhere, while the conspicuous bushy tail is dark grey with a white fringe.

The grey squirrel was introduced to Britain and Ireland in the nineteenth century from North America, where it is found in the hardwood forests of eastern Canada and the United States, from Ontario and New Brunswick down to Florida. Black squirrels, a dark-coloured or melanistic form rather than a different species, are commonly found in some parts of this range; I went to Niagara three years ago and saw many squirrels, all of which were black. Black squirrels are occasionally seen in the British Isles, but the dark colour doesn't seem to worry either animal, as grey and black interbreed successfully.

Red squirrels are smaller than their grey cousins; they are the only diurnal tree squirrel in continental Europe, living wherever there are coniferous forests and broad-leaved woodlands, particularly in beech woods. In most parts of Europe there are black forms of the red squirrel, just as there are melanistic grey squirrels. The two forms occur together in the same population and interbreed; the ratio of dark to red animals varies from place to place. In autumn, throughout most of its range, the red squirrel moults to a dull greyish brown, it develops prominent ear-tufts and the tail becomes bushier and darker; but in northern Scandinavia the entire winter coat may fade to almost pure silver-grey. The ears and tail of both squirrel species are very important balancing organs, besides being expressive signalling devices; for example, the ears are laid back as a sign of aggression and stick up as a sign of defence.

Red squirrels spend most of their time in the tree-tops, only coming down to ground level to search for windfall cones or fungi. Having found food, the squirrel seeks out a tree stump or rock on which to sit, so that it can maintain a look-out while eating.

Both red and grey squirrels have two breeding seasons: one in summer, June to August, the other in winter, December to March. The squirrels born early in the year have a greater chance of surviving their first full winter, as by the time the cold weather arrives they are bigger than the summer brood and better able to fend for themselves. Squirrel courtship rituals involve display and racing and chasing among the branches, along the ground and up the trees. The male that first catches the female mates with her and the other males then leave her alone. The female repairs or enlarges a drey, or sometimes uses a hollow tree, for her nursery nest, lining it with soft, warm material such as grass, moss, shredded bark, and feathery seed heads and sheep's wool if these are available. There is a gestation period of five to six weeks before three to six young are born, blind, deaf and naked. Female squirrels are good mothers and care for their babies for about sixteen weeks, by which time the young are completely independent.

WINTER INSECTS

When out walking near my home at any time of the year, I come across dancing swarms of gnats. It is surprising, though, to see them on calm, sunlit days in winter, as they jig up and down as though trying to keep warm. Winter gnats, sometimes called winter craneflies, members of the family Trichoceridae, are about at other times of the year, but are easily overlooked when there are so many other insects around. However, even in winter there is a purpose to this dancing display, which is performed by a group of males: the insects set out to attract any wandering female of the same species who might happen along. Occasionally a female does turn up, and without further ado, she mates with one of the males and flies away; meanwhile the rest of the group dances on.

Moths may be seen in the headlights of the car, even in winter; these hardy insects belong to a select group, which includes the scarce umber, mottled umber, dotted border, pale brindled beauty, March moth and the winter moth, *Operophtera brumata*. The males are all winged, while the females only have vestigial wings – tiny rudimentary ruffles – and are unable to fly.

The winter moth, mottled umber and March moth lay eggs on the spurs of ornamental crabs and cherries, and on fruit trees; as the females are flightless, they have to climb up to a suitable spot. To stop them, gardeners fasten a grease band around the tree trunk in autumn, about 60 cm (2 ft) from the ground. The greasy substance traps the female moths as they attempt to climb the tree; the band may have to be

winter moth

replaced in January or February, but it is an effective deterrent to the flightless females. Otherwise, at dusk, during a mild spell in winter, the female moths emerge from the soil, walk to the foot of the chosen tree and begin to climb. Meanwhile, the male moths, which have been sheltering in the leaf litter, become aware of the pheromones – the scent released by the unfertilized females – and fly to the tree trunks to waylay and mate with the females as they ascend. After mating, the females lay their eggs in fissures in the bark, in the encrusting lichens growing on it or on the spurs of fruit trees; and there they remain until spring. When the eggs hatch, the tiny caterpillars look for juicy, tender, unfurling leaves upon which to feast; this is all well and good in a normal year, but when spring is late arriving the caterpillars die of hunger. This has an effect on the bird population, too, as they rely on finding many caterpillars for their young among the opening leaves.

SIGNS OF LIFE IN WINTER

When you are out walking, it is often easy to identify a number of different species of birds; but mammals are usually more difficult to spot. The reasons are fairly simple: there are more bird species than mammal species, and birds are more active by day, while mammals are usually lively at dusk or by night, remaining well hidden when there are people around during the day.

However, mammals, like birds, leave tracks and trails behind them, and these can tell you a lot about the habits, behaviour and diet of those elusive creatures. There are many clues to look for; and if you are patient and observant you will soon be able to find the signs that tell of hidden nests, feeding areas, food caches, meeting grounds or resting areas, and to discover which animal left the droppings or made the footprints.

An animal becomes thoroughly acquainted with its own home range and doesn't usually roam very far afield – although of course territories vary enormously in size from species to species. Predators wander considerable distances in search of their prey, but herbivores stay close to the safety of their home refuge. There are unseen boundaries that keep each animal within its own range, and the territory itself has boundary markings of some kind, such as droppings, urine scents or glandular

Deciphering the tracks and traces left by animals in the snow can be fascinating. A track means a set of footprints, while a trace may be any other sign of a creature's presence, such as a feather, a dropping or some partly eaten food. With a bit of practice, you will be able to deduce which animal has left each clue.

secretions, which deter other animals of the same species from entering. Each territory includes a place where the animal sleeps, cleans and grooms itself. This could be a burrow, a cavity in a tree or rock, a dense thicket or a nest – anywhere that the animal feels safe.

Animals cannot hide their movements when there is snow on the ground; at this time many of them are hungry, so they are out and about searching for food. On a fine day, after snow, the warmth of the sun penetrates the snow layer and warms the ground. The snow lying next to the ground melts and a cavity is formed; here grass and other low-growing plants are not frozen, and so are available to mice and voles, which are able to feed away from the eyes of hawks and owls. Deer and rabbits dig through the snow to reach this vegetation, too.

TRACKS

When there is 2–3 cm (about 1 in) of snow on the ground, and it is crisp with frost, animal tracks are clear and sharp. Rabbit and hare tracks are commonly seen in fields and in the shelter of hedges; they are quite similar in appearance, the hare's being larger and more widely spaced than those of the rabbit. The width of the hare's hind-foot track is about the same as that of a standard matchbox, while a rabbit's is only about two-thirds that width. When hopping, the four footprints of the rabbit and hare show the hind prints drawn up close behind those of the forefeet; when the animals are moving fast, the hind feet appear in front of the forefeet.

Red fox tracks are easily confused with those of a dog of similar size, but a fox's pad marks are smaller and not as close together as a dog's. The two central toe pads lie further forwards in the fox track and, particularly in northern areas, the hair between the pads grows dense and blurs the track. A badger's footprints are quite distinctive as it moves with a heavy tread; the large, bear-like tracks show five long claws on the forefeet and five shorter claws on the hind feet.

Cats walk on their toes. They have five toes on each forefoot and four on each hind foot, but the inner toe of the forefoot is positioned high so that it leaves no track. The footprint is almost circular in shape and does not show claw marks, as the claws are retracted when the cat is walking.

Squirrels move by hopping, and their tracks are found in close-knit groups of four. The two footprints close together at the back of the group are those of the forefeet, which show only four toes; the tracks of the hind feet show five toes, and are a little to the front of the group; they lie further apart and turn slightly outwards.

Small rodents, such as mice and voles, have four toes on each forefoot and five on each hind foot. Their tracks show the toes of the front feet splayed out, while the middle three toes of each hind foot are quite close together and the outer toes are splayed. It is difficult to identify the species of these little mammals, so look as well for feeding signs and droppings, which may give some clue to the animal's identity.

Birds tread only on their toes; a bird's foot never has more than four toes, of which three usually face forwards and one backwards. The exceptions to this include the swift, whose four toes all face forwards, enabling it to cling to almost vertical surfaces; and woodpeckers, whose two forward- and two backward-facing toes help them to climb the bark of trees. Running birds, such as the partridge, have only a stub of a hind toe, which keeps to a minimum the area of foot that comes in contact with the ground. In swimming birds, the upper surface of each foot has a web, a leathery fold of skin usually joining the three forward-pointing toes, while the hind toe has been reduced. Again there are some exceptions: the cormorant and the shag have all four toes webbed, while the coot and the grebes have lobed webs on each individual toe. A bird moves on the ground by hopping, walking or running; a hopping bird leaves tracks in pairs, while a walking bird produces a zigzag track or a straight line and a running bird, like other fast-moving animals, has a longer length of stride.

IN A NUTSHELL

Nutshells give away the presence of small mammals. Hazelnuts have hard shells and each animal which eats them has its own way of getting the nut out of the shell. Squirrels split the hazelnut lengthwise into two clean halves by holding it between the forefeet and gnawing a groove across the top until they have made a small hole. They then insert their lower incisors into the hole and use them like a crowbar to split the nut.

Wood mice gnaw a hole into the side of the nut by holding it pressed to the ground and inclined inwards towards the chest. Having made a hole in the shell, the mouse inserts its lower incisors while holding its upper teeth against the outside of the shell; it then gnaws at the side away from its body. As the mouse turns the nut, the upper teeth leave a row of pale marks on the shell and the edge of the hole is irregular, as though it had been crumbled away.

A bank vole also holds the nut pressed against the ground, but it tucks the nut underneath itself, with the tip pointing away from the body. After making a hole in the shell, the vole inserts its snout, presses its upper incisors against the inner wall of the shell and gnaws at the nut with its lower incisors. This method does not leave teethmarks on the outside of the shell, and the edge of the hole is smooth and regular.

DROPPINGS AND PELLETS

Each individual species produces characteristic droppings. Herbivores – plant eaters – make many droppings that are usually small and round, while carnivores – meat eaters – produce fewer droppings, or faeces, that are often cylindrical with a point at one end. Badgers use special latrines about 10 cm (4 in) deep which they scrape out close to the sett. Foxes use their strongly smelling faeces to mark their territory, usually dropping them on a tree stump, a tussock of grass or a rock. Droppings contain the indigestible parts of food, such as hair, feathers, splinters of bone, the hard wing-cases of insects, known as chitin, and plant material. An examination of droppings will tell you what the animal has been feeding on; the bones, feathers and fur in the faeces of a carnivore can provide evidence of the prey species to be found in the area.

Many birds, including owls, gulls, crows, herons and magpies, get rid of those parts of their food which they are unable to digest by regurgitating them in compressed pellets. In birds, the part of the alimentary canal lying above the stomach cavity is usually formed into a thick-walled gizzard; in birds which produce pellets, those parts of the food that are indigestible accumulate here. They are pressed together into a pellet and, when this fills the gizzard, mucus is secreted to hold the pellet together and to help its passage out of the bird's throat.

The size of the pellet so produced is determined by the diameter of the bird's gullet – the oesophagus – so it will vary according to the species of bird. Examination of the food remains found in the pellets will give information on what a bird has been eating. If you find a pellet, make a note of where you found it, for birds prefer particular habitats and the location will give you a clue as to the bird's species. Pellets may be found at a bird's nesting or roosting site or feeding area; most birds usually produce two pellets a day.

These are just a few descriptions of the animal tracks and trails that you might find while out walking. By following some of the tracks you may discover more about the struggle animals have to survive the winter. Animal tracks may lead to signs of an ambush, a scuffle or a death. When following the track of a bird you may see the wing-marks where a rapid take-off has been necessary, or you might find a few feathers that could mean a very close encounter with a predator – or worse. Gradually you will learn more and more of the art of interpreting tracks and trails. This practice has roots deep in prehistory, when early man hunted his food by first learning the habits of his prey.

snowdrops

THE AWAKENING YEAR

A new and vital season arises from the harsh winter, born of the death of the old year.

EARLY FLOWERS

Suddenly, one day in February or March, there seems to be an intangible something in the air. Green shoots start to push their way through the debris at the bottom of the hedgerow and a vague mauve mist begins to soften the stark outline of trees and bushes. There may be a solitary daisy, a pink-tipped, white-petalled 'day's eye', shining out from a frosted lawn, or a yellow-flowered groundsel growing at the edge of a path; but the leader of the floral pageant is the snowdrop.

Snowdrops, despite being called, among other things, 'February's maids', begin to appear in January; they pierce through the snow or battle their way through dead leaves to open the dainty white, green-edged flowers which brighten the dullest day. They look so frail, hanging their heads from slender stalks, but they must be tough to be able to withstand the frost and snow.

Winter aconites also come into flower in January and February; they are often found in gardens, so you may have the opportunity to examine them. Like the hellebores I described in the previous chapter, they belong to the buttercup family, Ranunculaceae, and their floral structure is similar to that of the hellebore, although the colour is quite different. The shiny yellow-gold sepals are large and conspicuous in order to attract insects, while the petals are tubular structures which hold nectar; each flower is surrounded by a ruff of leaf-like bracts which protect the flower while it is in bud.

Most herbaceous plants are still dormant at this time of the year and wait until spring or summer to flower, when there are many pollinators about; but the plants that bloom so early, exposing their flowers to the rigours of frost and cold, do not depend entirely upon insect pollination for seed production. These early flowers are able to self-fertilize, using their own pollen, so producing new plants that are exactly like the parent. This means that any faults are also passed on, which is a disadvantage, like inbreeding in animals and humans. The early-flowering plants also have structures which can multiply and produce new plants; so barren strawberry, ground ivy, wood violet and dog's mercury are able to spread over the ground by means of stolons or creeping rootstocks.

These plants were all originally woodland-dwellers; and this might give a clue as to why they flower so early in the year. In a woodland habitat it is expedient to grow and flower before the leaves unfurl on the trees and cut out the light; also, at this time of the year the temperature of the leaf-covered woodland soil is considerably higher than that of open fields. The perennating structures, such as bulbs, corms and starchy roots, can store food, enabling the plants to produce flowers early in the year; these structures also provide winter food for mice and voles, as gardeners will know!

Many spring flowers are not pollinated by bees, which emerge relatively late, but by moths, flies and beetles. This explains why many spring flowers are pale in colour; for these colours show up well in the twilight, when moths are feeding. The primrose, for example, stays open all night, its pale face shining from a dark background of leaves; bee flies visit the flower by day and moths feed from it at dusk.

WIND-BLOWN

Some trees flower very early in the year, when their leaves are still tightly furled in bud. The hazel opens its dangling male catkins, or 'lamb's tails', and spreads the tiny plumes of the bud-like female flowers in February. Each catkin consists of a chain of male flowers; each flower has two tiny bracts and a single flower of four stamens – although there appear at first sight to be eight, as the stems divide to make room for the pollen sacs. The female flower is like a miniature green helmet, with a plume of twelve sticky scarlet stigmas protruding from the top.

Of the elms, the wych elm is usually the first to flower, in late February or early March; the flowers are in clusters, like purple-red tufts on the bare twigs. Each flower has five sepals, five stamens with purplish-red anthers and two sticky styles to catch passing pollen.

The alder flowers early in March, the long male catkins blowing in the wind, with the short, club-like female catkins just above them. The dark, empty, cone-like fruits of previous years hang on the trees for several seasons, making the alder easy to identify.

These early-flowering trees do not need to attract insects for pollination; instead they welcome the wind, for they are wind-pollinated. This is an effective method of pollination when insects are scarce, but it requires a great deal of pollen to be shed into the wind, in the hope that some grains will land on the tiny, sticky stigmas of female flowers of other trees in the same

hazel catkins

species. On a mild, breezy day in late winter or early spring, you may see clouds of pollen being carried from these trees; and certainly if you take a catkin-bearing twig into the house you will see how much pollen falls from the stamens. The pollen grains of wind-pollinated plants have a smooth, dry surface so that the wind can carry one or two grains away at a time – whereas the sticky, ornamented pollen of insect-pollinated plants clusters in groups.

In late March, the well-known, erect 'pussy-willow' catkins begin to open. These are the flowers of *Salix caprea*, the tree the British call pussy willow and the Americans goat willow; it is also sometimes known as sallow. They are often gathered to decorate churches on Palm Sunday, the Sunday before Easter, instead of the real palm leaves of warmer countries. Goat willow trees are either male or female; female trees bear pale green catkins and offer nectar to insects, while male trees carry the velvety grey 'pussy' catkins, which erupt with stamens full of golden pollen. These catkins may be wind-pollinated, but so many insects feed from them that they are usually insect-pollinated.

OVERWINTERING BEES

Bees are extremely important insects as they are the major pollinators of flowering plants. Without bees there would be fewer seeds and therefore fewer plants.

In Britain, honey bees are the first bees to appear in spring. They are followed by the first queen bumble bees and then the early solitary bees. Although these bees have varied tongue lengths, they all feed from the nectar and pollen of the goat willow and from the early flowers of coltsfoot and dandelion.

Solitary bees overwinter as pupae, tucked up in holes in well-drained soil, in walls or in wood, where they are put as eggs by a mother who does not survive long enough to see her offspring.

Each autumn, bumble bee colonies die of cold and starvation, leaving behind fertilized queens who hibernate alone throughout the winter, to establish new colonies in spring. The young bumble bee queen chooses a site for hibernation in autumn; it is often a north-facing bank which will not be warmed by the winter sun, so that she will not wake up too early. Here she burrows several centimetres (an inch or two) into the soil and overwinters, living on accumulated fat. By the time the soil temperature rises in spring most of this food reserve has been used up and the bee emerges to sun herself, warming her muscles before foraging for pollen and nectar among the early flowers; the food helps her ovaries to begin to develop.

Look out for the large bumble bee queens visiting the flowers of pussy willow, white deadnettle or flowering currant; and watch as the bees search for a suitable nesting site, flying to and fro over banks and rough ground, exploring holes and disappearing under tussocks of grass. Bumble bee queens look for established nest sites which will save them time and energy; they seem to favour old mouse holes and vole holes and they will sometimes be persuaded to nest in an upturned earthenware plant pot if it has some mousey-smelling nesting material in it. Having prepared a suitable site, the queen bumble bee begins to found a colony of bees that will forage for pollen and nectar – and so pollinate flowers – until autumn.

I used to keep honey bees and was able to watch a small colony in an observation hive; their winter behaviour was fascinating. Honey bees are perennial; they live through the winter, keeping each other warm and gradually eating up their reserves of honey. They survive because of their ability to collect pollen and nectar in excess of their immediate needs, and to turn the nectar into storable honey.

In summer, worker honey bees live for only five or six weeks; but winter bees are quite different. In autumn the worker bees feed well on pollen in order to build up a considerable amount of fat, protein and animal starch, known as glycogen, which is stored in large cells lining the top or dorsal side of the abdomen. In this way the lifespan of the winter bee is extended to help the colony live through the winter.

When the temperature outside the hive falls to about 18°C (64°F), honey bees begin to form small groups; when the temperature inside the hive falls to 13°C (55°F), the groups begin to gather into small clusters and then into a ball, encompassing more and more of the honey combs as it grows, until there is one mass of bees clinging together on the combs. Each bee's rear end is turned to the outside of the cluster and the bees pack themselves closer and closer together, so maintaining a temperature of about 20–30°C (70–85°F) within the cluster; the rate of heat loss is lowered by the reduction in the surface area of the closely packed bodies. The bees in the centre of the cluster eat honey and turn it into heat energy which is shared by all the bees. The loss of heat can be regulated by the expansion and contraction of the cluster and by increasing or decreasing the consumption of honey, so the clustered colony has control of its temperature. The bees that cling to the outside of the bottom of the cluster are the coldest of the

In spring, when flowers open and small animals emerge into the warm sunshine, birds begin their courtship. This male wren is collecting lichen to line his nest.

group; they are exposed to the temperature of the hive itself and if the cluster cools and these bees find themselves in a temperature as low as 8°C (46°F), then they become comatose, fall off and die.

During the winter, the honey eaten has to be diluted and bees go out of the hive when possible to collect water. The few that brave the cold fly out, quickly fill up with water and return to the hive as fast as they can to regurgitate the water. When the weather is too severe for them to venture outside, honey is diluted with liquid from the bees' thoracic and salivary glands. Water is also produced by the bees at the centre of the cluster, which become very warm and release water vapour; this is drawn into the spiracles – pores – of the surrounding bees and absorbed into their tissues.

When the outside temperature rises, the worker bees are tempted out to forage and gradually, as spring gets under way, the hive returns to normal and the queen begins to lay again.

EARTH WORKS

Moles are busy miners of the soil. They live in darkness and solitude, constructing complicated tunnel systems at various levels in the earth. The mole does most of its feeding when it is patrolling along its burrows, as these act as a sort of pit-fall trap, into which earthworms, insects and soil invertebrates drop, to be picked up and eaten while they are still bemused. More tunnels are excavated to increase the size of the feeding area, and the loose soil that accumulates from this activity is pushed above ground, making a molehill. In order to get rid of the unwanted loose soil, the mole digs a vertical shaft to the surface and pushes the spoil upwards and outwards. If you have ever seen a molehill being made, you will have seen the amount of soil that can be pushed out from the tunnel system in quite a short time. I once timed a mole making a hill; it took eighteen minutes to finish pushing up the spoil from the shaft, and the soil so displaced weighed about 4.3 kg (9$^{1}/_{2}$ lb), which is more than forty times the weight of an average mole. All the time these excavations were erupting from the ground, a robin was busily feeding on worms and other creatures in the loose soil.

A mole's system of burrows includes one or more nests, lined with grass or dead leaves, in which the animal rests every four hours or so. There is a path of stone slabs leading to the door of our cottage, and I have often been watching through the window when a mole has appeared from between two slabs; one day it popped up time and again to reach out for leaves to carry down to line a nest. Another time I found a

elm flowers

newly dead mouse and put
it by the hole that the
mole used to sur-
face; soon after-
wards, I saw the
body of the mouse disappearing down the hole.

alder catkins

During very cold weather in winter, molehills appear above the snow, or above ground that is frozen as hard as stone. This would at first appear to suggest that moles are able to dig frozen soil; but in reality the mole is digging in the soft, warmer layers of soil, below the area that is frozen, and the spoil is being pushed up through pre-existing shafts. Earthworms, insects and soil animals retreat deeper into the soil in winter to escape being immobilized by the cold; so the mole also moves into deeper, warmer burrows where food is more likely to be available.

A fall of snow warms the top layer of soil; and moles that have retreated into deep tunnels, during periods of hard frost, may move upwards to the comparatively shallow layers when snow has fallen. As you go for a walk on snowy days, watch out for runs in the area where the soil and the snow meet; they are fairly obvious on meadow-land when the snow is not too deep.

Usually when moles meet they fight; but during February the male mole searches for a mate. A female will repulse a mole until she becomes sexually receptive, and then there is a brief, peaceful encounter when the moles push their aggression to one side and mate. After a few hours the male returns to his own territory, the future of the mole species having been ensured.

At this time of the year, too, there are many molehills to be seen. A thaw brings about great activity, and a rash of earth mounds appear; in poor soil, the mole has to enlarge the underground territory constantly to look for enough food to live on. If a mole is hungry, it will come out on to the ground surface to forage for earthworms, insects or carrion. It is very vulnerable at this time and may fall victim to owls, herons, foxes or badgers; but its greatest enemy is man. So saying, I must add that I am very fond of moles and enjoy watching their above-ground activities; moreover, I find the soil from molehills perfect for pot plants.

EARLY RISING

In early spring, when the sun is warm, reptiles and amphibians gradually begin to emerge from their winter torpor. Slow-worms – which are not worms, but legless lizards – adders and grass snakes begin to

make a move in March or April, while sand lizards and smooth snakes sleep a little longer. Frogs usually wake up in March, but the month can vary from January in the south of their range to April in the north. It is dangerous for a frog to wake up too early. Sometimes the frogs which have chosen to overwinter in the protective mud at the bottom of a pond wake in early spring only to find that the water surface is frozen over; then many die from lack of oxygen.

The ancestors of modern frogs, toads and newts were the first animals with backbones to leave the sea and live in wet places on land. These pioneers had rudimentary lungs and leg-like fins; over many, many years their legs gradually evolved, enabling the animals to compete better for food and to move from one watery site to another. The lungs of amphibians have now become adequate for breathing in atmospheric oxygen, while their skin has retained the ability to absorb oxygen from water; but their early development has not evolved to the same extent. The eggs laid by amphibians resemble fish spawn, and the larval stage, in the form of tadpoles, is similar to the early phase of young fish; so all amphibians must return to water to breed.

Amphibians today are divided into two groups: those with tails – newts and salamanders – and those without – frogs and toads. Besides their appearance, there is a difference in their mating behaviour and the way in which the eggs are fertilized. Newts and salamanders prefer a quiet, more solitary courtship and mating, while frogs and toads are noisy, gregarious and physical.

CROAKING A LOVE SONG

Many people eagerly await the arrival of frogs in their ponds in early spring and look for the floating masses of spawn, which are a sign that warmer weather is on the way.

Frogs and toads become sexually mature when they are three or four years old. Males of the common frog emerge from their winter retreats and begin to congregate in large numbers at various breeding sites, preferably on a mild, rainy night. It is an amazing sight to see the frogs arriving, diving into the water, then lifting their heads above the surface to strike up their chorus of croaks to attract the females. It is even more of a spectacle when the females arrive, because by then the males have worked themselves up into such a frenzy that the water appears to boil with frogs, frantic to mate. There are always more males than females, which leads to many fights, and an eager male who cannot find a female will clutch at a fish, a stick or another male frog in his excitement. A male who succeeds in grabbing a female wraps his front legs around her body, just below the 'armpits', and hangs on to her in a position called amplexus. The pair remain linked until the female has laid her 2000 or so eggs and the male has released his sperm to fertilize them externally. The female usually leaves the pond after spawning to feed and build up her strength, while the male looks around for another mate.

Common toads are a little later leaving their winter hide-aways and are more particular about their breeding sites, preferring to deposit their strings of eggs in deep water. They may have to travel quite a distance to the water of their choice, so males and females often converge on the pond together; many females are waylaid en route and complete the journey with a male firmly attached in amplexus. Grabbing a female in this way does not mean that a male has the right to her; larger males, with deep, resonant croaks, are strong contestants and a small male does not fight for his captured female for long.

When the female is ready to lay, she slowly releases up to 7000 eggs in a long string; the male fertilizes these as they are extruded. The string of eggs can be 2-3 metres (6–10 ft) long, and it is carefully entwined around the stems of water plants before the female toad leaves the pond.

Each of the eggs of a frog or toad is enveloped in jelly and, once they have been deposited in the water, the jelly swells to insulate the egg from the coldness of the water and the atmosphere. Should the weather be cold, the eggs will be slow to develop; but if the weather is mild, then the eggs develop quickly. Many eggs are laid, but not all of them hatch; the tadpoles and the young frogs and toads that do develop face many hazards and only a few survive to adulthood.

SHALL WE DANCE?

Newts and salamanders do not attract a mate by calling; instead the newts perform an underwater courtship, while female salamanders are wooed on land.

Newts usually spend the winter hibernating in leaf litter, under rocks, beneath logs, or in the cracks and crevices of old walls. On a mild, damp evening in late March or April they migrate from their winter hiding places to ponds, where the courtship rituals take place. The intriguing sequence of the mating rites varies from species to species, but the basic principles are the same.

When a male newt meets a female he swims around her, undulating his dorsal crest, which is splendid in the breeding season; he sniffs at the female's genital opening, known as the cloaca, probably to assess her breeding condition. The female usually swims away, feigning indifference, but not going far. The male takes up a position in front of her, raising his crest and fanning his tail backwards and forwards along his body, driving his smell towards her. He becomes more and more excited and begins to butt the female's sides with his head; she takes her time and it is not until she is quite ready that she responds by moving towards the male. He retreats, still displaying. If the female continues to follow, the male turns and creeps away from her; the female follows and touches his tail with her snout. This is the signal for the male to deposit a packet of sperm – the spermatophore – on the mud; he creeps away from it slowly, his tail folded along his side, and moving only far enough to ensure that, when the female moves forward to touch his tail again, she will stop with her cloaca above the spermatophore. She stops as planned, and the sperm packet is drawn up into the female's body. This wonderful sequence may be repeated two or three times to ensure fertilization, but many sequences are aborted when the partners lose interest or are distracted.

A few days later the female begins to lay eggs. Each individual egg is put on to a leaf and the leaf is folded over in protection; it takes a few days for the female to lay about 300 eggs so carefully. The tadpoles of newts are beautiful; they have long, frilled, external gills that wave in the water as the tadpoles dart about. The gills are retained until the youngsters are almost ready to leave the water, when they are absorbed. The tiny front legs develop a week or so after hatching and are soon followed by the hind legs.

Salamanders mate on land after hibernating. Their mating is sometimes rough and ready, involving much chasing, nudging and occasional biting. Fertilization is brought about by means of a sperm packet which is taken into the cloaca of the female for internal fertil-ization, as with newts. However, the young salamanders are not born for some time; indeed, the gestation period may be up to a year, according to the species. The female enters shallow water to give birth to as many as twenty – sometimes fifty – live young. Salamander tadpoles are very like those of newts, with external gill-tufts and a well-developed tail.

REBUILDING POPULATIONS

As the days lengthen and the sun begins to warm the earth, biological clocks ring out the news that spring is here at last. Many animals will not have survived the privations of winter, but the breeding season is in sight, and with it comes a chance to rebuild populations. By March, buds are swelling and insects are on the move; the lengthening days give more time for foraging and for getting into good condition for the hard work facing those animals with families to raise.

Some birds, including the mallard, great crested grebe and herring gull, form pairs before finding a territory, while the males of some species, such as robins, wrens, marsh tits and blackbirds, defend a

Garlic mustard is one of the food plants of orange-tip butterflies.

territory throughout the winter. There are some birds that pair for life – these are usually long-lived birds such as the fulmar, shag, gannet, goose and jackdaw; but most pair with a different mate each breeding season. Male wrens living in rich woodland areas, or other habitats where there is plenty of food, are polygamous, while those living in poorer areas are monogamous. We once had three wrens' nests in the garden and we were able to see how the male divided his time and his foraged food between them.

It is usually the male bird who is responsible for establishing and defending a territory, while the females build up their energy by eating nutritious food, to be ready for egg-laying and incubation. Competition between birds for territory, nest sites, food and mates causes hostility, which in its turn sparks aggression and fear, but rarely full-blooded fighting. Birds use bluff, bluster, threats and physical displays to drive away their rivals. Having established a territory the bird displays itself visually and vocally. Many male birds have distinctive colouring during the breeding season. The bill of both the male and female puffin becomes red, yellow and blue; male pheasants are splendid, with erect ear-tufts and inflated red facial wattles; chaffinches, thrushes and the usually drab sparrows become brighter, with more distinctive markings.

Birds communicate several things vocally. For instance, they use repetitive jarring sounds to warn of danger or drive away a rival; with a few notes a bird is able to state its species, or pass on the news of where food may be found; but when it comes to attracting a mate or defending a territory, the male bird sings a complex arrangement of notes that is music to human ears, repelling intrusion from other males and arousing the attention of unmated females. Territorial songs are loud and clear; the less conspicuous a bird's plumage, the louder his song seems. Birds living in dense vegetation have loud songs, too. These songs are persistent, repeated over and over again, from the first light of dawn to the last flicker of light at dusk. It is lovely to hear a bird singing, but it can drive you wild to hear 'a little bit of bread and no-o-o cheese' hundreds of times a day. There was once a blackbird nesting in our garden which used to sing the tune and the word-rhythm of the phrase 'somewhere over the rainbow'; it was the only song my family sang for weeks, it invaded our minds so much!

Many bird species sing from a song-post, which may be the upper branches of a tree, the gable end of a house or the top of a telegraph pole – any raised position that will help the sound carry over a wide area. Others, such as larks, rise high into the sky, singing as they go, while the whitethroat and the pipit perform a sort of aerial dance as they sing their territorial songs. More birds sing for about half an hour around dawn than at any other time in the day; and the dawn chorus gathers in strength as the spring does.

It is very important for birds to hold a territory, for this disperses the birds more widely within a suitable habitat, reducing the competition for food and for nesting and roosting sites. Once within their own territory, a pair of birds can mate with little interference from rivals, and their joint defence of the territory helps to strengthen the pair bond. The spacing out of nests in a territorial system probably makes it more difficult for predators to find them, as each nest can be built in the best place for concealment in the vicinity.

A mammal's territory is only part of its home range – the area over which it forages and feeds. Most animals try to defend their nest site from intruders, this being their personal territory; mammals use scent markers to indicate the area individuals regard as their own, and other animals of the same species usually stay away. Scent markers may persist for weeks, and the sensitive noses of other animals are able to decipher the messages that have been left; information about the sex, breeding condition and social status of the owner of the territory, all wrapped up in faeces, droppings, spraints, urine or glandular secretions.

Mammals usually only defend their territory from others of the same species, as different species exploit different resources within the home range, so do not often compete; but when two species' resource requirements overlap, there is likely to be conflict. For example, if a shrew is hunting along its own runs in the grass and meets a mouse or a vole, it will react aggressively, trying to shoo the other animal away. However, it is when the resident shrew meets another shrew on its 'patch' that there is real trouble: then, the scolding, 'shrewish' behaviour of the territory holder is loud and long, and may end in a fight.

When the owner of a territory dies, the speed at which the site is taken over by a newcomer shows how efficiently potential settlers are kept at bay by the presence of the resident animal. It is also an indication of how territorial behaviour limits population density. It is the stronger, better qualified individuals that win a territory and breed, while the less well-equipped fail to breed and die.

I hope that this book will help you to look at the winter season in a new light. What I have tried to show you is that, if a plant or animal is going to survive and reproduce successfully, it has to fit in with its environment; if it does not, it will cease to exist. Every plant or animal which faces a season of cold weather with little food must have all the adaptations necessary for winter survival; for it is only in this way that its species will live to play its part in the great web of life.

Lenten rose

INDEX